A BIBLIOGRAPHY OF THE
WRITINGS OF
HENRY JAMES

Chocorua, N. H.
Sept: 8 1904

Dear Sir,

I am afraid I am
really not able to help or
enlighten you in respect to
the matter on which I
just receive your letter
the question of a "Bibliography" of my production,
early & late. You see
authors in general do

...must
accept all manner
of congruences, but
they must at least
keep their hands from
the pick-axe & the
spade. My own impres-
sion is that I have
hitherto got off well,
& have been very little
bibliographized for

... will find themselves
interested in a miraculously
complete resuscitation
of their writings — there
being always, inevitably,
too many that they
desire to forget, to keep
buried. This leads them
to watch with some
detachment the process
of digging up ...

I have escaped positively
knowing of anything of
the sort as I have cer-
tainly escaped contributing
to it. If you so generously
enjoy the results I can
only congratulate you on
the test of your curiosity
— but I am at a loss
to give you any genial
assistance & am your
most truly
Henry James
Le Roy Phillips Esq.

A Bibliography

OF THE WRITINGS OF

Henry James

By

LeRoy Phillips

BURT FRANKLIN: BIBLIOGRAPHY AND REFERENCE SERIES #189

BURT FRANKLIN
NEW YORK

Published By
BURT FRANKLIN
235 East 44th St.
New York, N.Y. 10017

ORIGINALLY PUBLISHED
NEW YORK: 1930
Reprinted 1968

Printed in U.S.A.

Contents

Introduction

HENRY JAMES died in February, 1916. His literary activity, in an unwearied pursuit of excellence, had extended through a period of more than fifty years. The enumeration of his writings, early and late, has been attempted in the pages of this book.

In supplying bibliographical information, relative to his own work, Henry James was reluctant, sometimes inexact. The Prefaces (1907–9), with which he introduced twenty-four volumes of the New York edition of the *Novels and Tales*, held promise; but, for anyone concerned with the names of publishing firms and the dates when novels came from the press, they were disappointingly nebulous, reflecting the tone of the demurring letter of 1904, of which a facsimile accompanies this book. The Prefaces added little to the bibliographical data which was already available.

A published account of what Henry James had written prior to 1906 has long been out of print, and copies, as they turn up in auction sales or in dealers' catalogues, command a noticeable premium. After the appearance of that record of unfinished performance, ten years remained to the author, a decade which was to see him advance and receive the highest distinctions as a literary artist, both in the country of his birth and in that to which he transferred his allegiance during the first year of the Great War.

Henry James was sixty-two when the materials for the previous *Bibliography* were assembled. The editorial sponsors of his initial efforts were touching their threescore years and ten, and the files of old or extinct periodicals, in which the contributions of his youth had been printed, were becoming difficult to trace. The expediency of discovering, and bringing out from their obscurity, the earliest of the unsigned critical notes and reviews was only too apparent. Recalling the search of twenty-five years ago, and the diminishing number of those who, from their private knowledge, could give assistance, I doubt the likelihood of a "resuscitation," so "mercilessly complete," if we had waited until a later date.

Literary friends and associates who still had memoranda of the past in their keeping supplied a collection of facts beyond that which is usual in bibliographical records. From here and there came little-known, or unknown, bits of "inside information" and the *Bibliography of 1906*, of which this book is the extension and elaboration, became more than a perfunctory check list of an author widely read and beginning to be widely collected.

Among the many who helped in this way, I should ascribe a special indebtedness to the late Wendell Phillips Garrison. From the founding of the *Nation*, Mr. Garrison was the associate of E. L. Godkin, its first editor, and, after 1881,

was editor in charge until 1906. His personal
diary, painstakingly kept, disclosed that Henry
James, Jr., at the age of twenty-two, was an
anonymous reviewer for the *Nation's* initial number, July 6, 1865, and that he continued a fre-
quent, probably the youngest, contributor for
more than fourteen years.

The issue of the *Nation*, July 8, 1915, com-
memorating its half-century of continuous publication, printed a significant and singular retro-
spection under the caption,—"The Founders of
'The Nation.' Recollections of the 'Fairies' that
Attended Its Birth." We may believe this to be
the last of Henry James's contributions to periodicals, which appeared during his lifetime.

The plates of Henry James's earlier novels did
veteran service; some of them may still be in use.
While impression was following impression, occasional alterations of title-page imprints were being made, due to the vanishing of old publishing
firms, or to their absorption under new names: but
this *Bibliography* makes no attempt to report
these or successive issues from the same plates or
from the same standing type.

Henry James has shown that he was his own
severest critic, canceling and emending his text,
so that different editions of the same title may
show variations. An enumeration of such muta-
tions is not a bibliographer's responsibility, but
they cannot be ignored entirely. Some of the more
interesting alterations have been noticed.

The intention in Part I, "Original Works," is to describe, from first edition copies, the physical details of all published books in which the text is the exclusive work of the author.

No titles in Part I, or elsewhere, are described more than once, except to point out the differences between the first American and the first English editions, concerning the precedence of which there are, sometimes, divergent tastes and conflicting fancies.

With the earlier books by Henry James, which are universally labeled, classified, and catalogued as "American Fiction," "American Biography," and the like, there can be no dispute. But, by reason of his long residence in England, with the final renouncement of his American citizenship, and his close association with the London publishers, it is contended that, after 1880, or thereabout, the English imprints, in certain cases, came more directly under the author's personal supervision than those "Made in U.S.A.," and that these should, consequently, have the preference in collections of first editions.

There are, moreover, extremists who regard simultaneous publication in the two countries as they would a birth of twins. Whenever the imprint date of a title is the same, or approximately the same, on both sides of the Atlantic, they try to avoid uncertainties and believe that their position as collectors of Henry James becomes unassailable, only when they have his firsts,—Ameri-

can and English,—in pairs. It is only in cases of
such duality that a book having the same title is
twice collated.

Editions of a book subsequent to the first—by
that I mean impressions from reset type or from
plates molded from such type—are indicated by
the words, "The Same." They are recorded in
chronological sequence, following the more precise
and extended descriptions of the original issues.

The very large number of books for which
Henry James provided Forewords and Introduc-
tions, especially during his later years, show his
matchless aptitude for the appraisal of work
which was not his own. The list of these volumes,
with bibliographical data, from first edition
copies, and his translation of Daudet's *Port Tara-
scon*,—Henry James's first published translation,
—for which he also wrote a "Translator's Preface," comprise Part III in this *Bibliography*.

In Part II, "Contributions to Books," are descriptions of the earliest impressions of the volumes in which Henry James is the author of only
a part of the text and in which his particular contributions are here appearing in print for the first
time.

Editors and compilers of volumes, designed to
illustrate the efforts of successful literary crafts-
men, have often turned to Henry James for copy.
When they have made selections of his work from
already published books, the compilations cannot
be ranked as first editions. Brief notices of them

suffice for the purposes of this record. They are
grouped, with references to the volumes in which
the selected text was first printed, under "Contributions to Books."

Henry James's efforts in dramatic composition
have attracted a widening interest and much that
was obscure regarding them is being disclosed. All
of the then-known printed plays were included
under Original Works or Contributions to Periodicals in the *Bibliography of 1906*.

In the Appendix of this previous record, men-
tion was made of two plays, professionally produced, but of which no printed copies had then
been discovered—a dramatization of the novel,
The American and *Guy Domville*. Copies of
these rarities were found later. Mr. Paul Lemperley of Lakewood, Ohio, provides for these pages,
with other unique bibliographical data, a description of his copy of *The American*, *A Comedy in
Four Acts;* while a treasured example of *Guy
Domville. Play in Three Acts*, "Printed as
Manuscript for Private Circulation Only," has
been acquired for the Henry E. Huntington Library and Museum of San Marino, California.
Through the coöperation of the Curator, Mr.
Robert O. Schad, and Miss Mary Potter, of the
Research Staff of the Library, a description of the
latter play has become available.

Another play, *Daisy Miller*, *A Comedy*, "Not
Published,"—a stage version, in three acts, of the
author's like-named "Study," was never profes-

sionally produced. The copy of this comedy, from which a collation was made for the earlier *Bibliography*, and there included among "Original Works," is now in the Henry James Collection presented to the Library of Congress by Mrs. Sarah Jones. The author's dramatization of *Daisy Miller* was later edited for publication and appeared, as here recorded, in the *Atlantic Monthly* and in book form.

The printing of these unpublished plays was probably for purposes of copyright and to provide convenient prompt books for use in the theater. They are grouped together in this *Bibliography*, making Part IV, "Unpublished Dramatic Works."

In another way the three unpublished plays are in a class by themselves; their extreme rarity places the possession of them almost beyond the most ardent collector's aspiration.

Henry James made stage versions of several of his other novels and tales, of which a few were produced; but if there are printed copies of them, they are now unknown.

Since the author's death, there have been attempts to adapt his fiction for the theatre. Henry James's unfinished novel, *The Sense of the Past*, contained suggestions which John L. Balderston successfully recast for acting in *Berkeley Square* (1926). This play and a dramatization of *The Tragic Muse* (1927) by Hubert Griffith have been published.

The idea of including all of Henry James's published writings in a collective set would be appalling. A very considerable number of stories, characteristic efforts of his earlier period, which did not satisfy the author's later taste, the plays, and the non-fiction will, in all probability, never be assembled for a series of uniform volumes.

The New York edition of the *Novels and Tales*, in twenty-four volumes (1907–9), "included all of the author's fiction which he wished perpetuated." Two novels, which were unfinished at his death, were added (these supplementary volumes were printed from the plates of the first American editions) in 1918. A more comprehensive edition, including, besides the contents of the first twenty-four volumes of the New York edition, "all of the other fiction which Henry James put forth in book-form during his life," was published (1921–23) in thirty-five uniform volumes. Bibliographical records of these and of the minor collective editions, all fiction, are found in Part V.

The thickness of this *Bibliography* is considerably due to Part VI, "Contributions to Periodicals."

Most of the author's unsigned notes and reviews, dating from the late sixties and the seventies, were obscured in widely scattered journals, until they were pointed out in the *Bibliography of 1906*. Lately, an intensive examination has been made of them by readers who were attracted because of their authorship and by students of essays on the literature of the period.

There are instances among these anonymous contributions where variations from the author's conventional style of writing have been noted. In one arresting example, a book review, it is also indicated that the volume under consideration, scientific in subject, probably would not have been assigned to Henry James for criticism. That this review may be the work of William James is a suggestion, which the *Annotated Bibliography* of his writings by Ralph Barton Perry fails to confirm.

Clerical and typographical errors in compiling indexes are the main reasons for possible inaccuracies of attribution among the "Contributions to Periodicals." The discovery and reporting of them will be gratefully appreciated.

The subtle amenities of letter writing, which are exemplified in the two volumes edited by Percy Lubbock, are also revealed in the multiplying memoirs and biographies of Henry James's contemporaries, through which much of his correspondence is scattered. Among such recent books are *Edwin Austin Abbey. The Records of His Life and Work*, and *The Colvins and Their Friends*, both by E. V. Lucas; *Life in Letters by William Dean Howells*, edited by Miss Mildred Howells; and *J. William White, M.D. A Biography*, by Agnes Repplier. But to attempt to point out the innumerable detached letters now in type and attributed to Henry James would be supererogatory. Occasionally, in the form of a slender book or a brochure, some written communications by Henry James have been printed separately in very limited issues. These are necessarily included in a bibliography.

The concluding pages are a "List of Titles" of the work of Henry James as it has come to us in books and in periodicals,—an alphabetical table of reference to the maze of literary documents, novels, short tales, travel notes, essays, prefaces, biographies, book reviews, critical papers, groups of letters and plays,—in which the author reflected the color and texture of his time. The original and subsequent appearances of each title are recorded.

The book size terms here used are the common trade designations as given by the publishers in their descriptions of the various volumes. In the case of privately printed books and booklets the sizes are given in inches.

In their original condition, the books described between these covers are increasingly treasured. The constantly arising queries of the bibliophile were considered in the bringing together and arrangement of the previous record, and this extension of that effort, I am encouraged to believe, will be used by the survivors of the old guard of James's collectors and by new recruits.

My acknowledgment of assistance must fall short of what is due: librarians, publishers, booksellers, collectors, and readers have never disregarded an appeal for help. Searchings have been undertaken with enthusiasm and promptness in libraries and in privately owned collections.

Mr. Paul Lemperley, whose aid I have already mentioned, not only put his unrivaled collection of James firsts at my disposal, but, to every inquiry he made detailed reply, giving suggestions and supplying immediate information from letters of the author which are now in his keeping. Mrs. John Tucker Murray of Cambridge, Massachusetts, has allowed me to see volumes in her finely selected group of first editions, many of them from Henry James's own library. Among the treasures of other collections which I have examined are those belonging to Mr. H. B. Collamore of Hartford, Connecticut.

The Henry James Collection in the Library of Congress has been available through the unfailing coöperation of Mr. M. A. Roberts, Superintendent of the Reading Room. At the Widener Library of Harvard University I have had valuable assistance from Mrs. F. V. Livingston, who herself has made an exhaustive compilation of the published work of Henry James, and also from Mr. George Parker Winship and Mr. Walter B. Briggs. From the New York Public Library, Mr. H. M. Lydenberg has contributed titles and dates not reported previously. The collections of the Boston Athenaeum and the Boston Public Library have also been consulted. Miss Constance

Grosvenor Alexander of Wellesley, Massachusetts, made a special search for privately printed
material in the Library of the British Museum.

Gratitude must be expressed to Miss Lois L.
Comings of New York City, whose scholarly
study of the work of Henry James has been recog-
nized by Yale University. Miss Comings discovered at the Bibliothèque Nationale a signed and
published, but hitherto undetected, review of
Zola's *Nana*. In this instance M. de la Roncière
of the Bibliothèque Nationale gave friendly and
courteous aid.

The author of *An Introduction to Bibliography for Literary Students*, Mr. Ronald B. Mc-
Kerrow of London, has supplied facts without
which this record would be less complete.

I cannot leave unmentioned the help which I
have received from the late Brander Matthews of
Columbia University.

Mr. Henry James of New York City, as his
uncle's literary executor, has given consent to the
inclusion of a letter, here reproduced in facsimile.

On other pages of this book I have also noted a
part of my indebtedness to those who have contributed to its utility and scope.

LeRoy Phillips.

Boston, Massachusetts,
 July, 1930.

PART I

Original Works

With Descriptions of the First Editions
American and English
and
Notices of All Subsequent Editions

ORIGINAL WORKS

1875

A / PASSIONATE PILGRIM, / and Other Tales. / By / Henry James, Jr. / [publishers' device] / Boston: / James R. Osgood and Company, / Late Ticknor & Fields, and Fields, Osgood, & Co. / 1875.

12mo, pp. ii. 496, 2 blanks. Cloth.

Contents

A Passionate Pilgrim.
Originally appeared in the *Atlantic Monthly*, March–April, 1871.

The Last of the Valerii.
Originally appeared in the *Atlantic Monthly*, January, 1874.

Eugene Pickering.
Originally appeared in the *Atlantic Monthly*, October–November, 1874.

The Madonna of the Future.
Originally appeared in the *Atlantic Monthly*, March, 1873.

The Romance of Certain Old Clothes.
Originally appeared in the *Atlantic Monthly*, February, 1868.

Madame de Mauves.
Originally appeared in the *Galaxy*, February–March, 1874.

For reprintings of these tales in collective volumes, *see* the Index.

TRANSLATION

1876. Ein leidenschaftlicher Erdenpilger und an-

dere Erzählungen. Von Henry James jun. Ins
Deutsche übertragen von Moritz Busch.

Published in *Novellisten*, Amerikanische, Number 1.
Leipzig: Grunow.

TRANSATLANTIC SKETCHES. / By / Henry James, Jr. / [publishers' device] / Boston: / James R. Osgood and Company, / Late Ticknor & Fields, and Fields, Osgood, & Co. / 1875.

12mo, pp. [ii], vi. 7–401, 3 blanks. Cloth.

Contents

Chester.
Originally appeared in the *Nation*, July 4, 1872.

Lichfield and Warwick.
Originally appeared in the *Nation*, July 25, 1872.

North Devon.
Originally appeared in the *Nation*, August 8, 1872.

Wells and Salisbury.
Originally appeared in the *Nation*, August 22, 1872.

Swiss Notes.
Originally appeared in the *Nation*, September 19, 1872.

From Chambéry to Milan.
Originally appeared in the *Nation*, November 21, 1872.

From Venice to Strasburg.
Originally appeared in the *Nation*, March 6, 1873, where Strasburg is spelled "Strassburg."

The Parisian Stage.
Originally appeared in the *Nation*, January 9, 1873.

A Roman Holiday.
Originally appeared in the *Atlantic Monthly*, July, 1873.

Roman Rides.
Originally appeared in the *Atlantic Monthly*, August, 1873.

Roman Neighborhoods.
  Originally appeared in the *Atlantic Monthly*, December, 1873.

The After-Season in Rome.
  Originally appeared in the *Nation*, June 12, 1873.

From a Roman Note-Book.
  Originally appeared in the *Galaxy*, November, 1873.

A Chain of Cities.
  Originally appeared, under the title "A Chain of Italian Cities," in the *Atlantic Monthly*, February, 1874.

The St. Gothard.
  Originally appeared, under the title "An Autumn Journey," in the *Galaxy*, April, 1874.

Siena.
  Originally appeared in the *Atlantic Monthly*, June, 1874.

The Autumn in Florence.
  Originally appeared in the *Nation*, January 1, 1874.

Florentine Notes.
  Originally appeared, in eight instalments, in the *Independent* in 1874;—under the above title, April 23, 30, and May 21;—under the title, "A Florentine Garden," May 14;—under the title, "Old Italian Art," June 11;—under the title, "Florentine Architecture," June 18;—under the title, "An Italian Convent," July 2;—under the title, "The Churches of Florence," July 9.

Tuscan Cities.
  Originally appeared in the *Nation*, May 21, 1874.

Ravenna.
  Originally appeared in the *Nation*, July 9, 1874.

The Splügen.
  Originally appeared, under the title "A Northward Journey," in the *Independent*, August 20–27, 1874.

Homburg Reformed.
  Originally appeared in the *Nation*, August 28, 1873.

Darmstadt.
  Originally appeared, under the title "An Ex-Grand-Ducal Capital," in the *Nation*, October 9, 1873.

In Holland.
Originally appeared in the *Nation*, August 27, 1874.
In Belgium.
Originally appeared in the *Nation*, September 3, 1874.

Foreign Parts, published 1883, is largely a reprint of *Transatlantic Sketches*. In the later volume the following papers are omitted,—The Parisian Stage, The After-Season in Rome, The Autumn in Florence, The Splügen, and Parts II, VI, VII, and VIII of Florentine Notes.
English Hours, published 1905, includes the first four papers in *Transatlantic Sketches*.
Italian Hours, published 1909, includes several papers in *Transatlantic Sketches*. These, in some instances, were extended and amended for the later volume.

For reprintings of these papers in collective volumes, *see* the Index.

1876

RODERICK HUDSON. / By / Henry James, Jr. / [publishers' device] / Boston: / James R. Osgood and Company, / Late Ticknor & Fields, and Fields, Osgood, & Co. / 1876.
12mo, pp. vi. 482, 4 blanks. Cloth.

Originally appeared in the *Atlantic Monthly*, January–December, 1875.

THE SAME. 1879. *Revised and First English Edition*. Three volumes.

London: Macmillan and Co.

Note on page iii. "*Roderick Hudson* was first published in Boston, in 1875. It has now been minutely revised, and has received a large number of verbal alterations. Several passages have been rewritten."

THE SAME. 1879.

Published in *Collection of British Authors*, Volumes 1842 and 1843. Leipzig: Bernhard Tauchnitz.

THE SAME. 1880.

London: Macmillan and Co.

In 1882, as a "Revised Edition," sheets of this edition were imported for America and published with the imprint of Houghton, Mifflin and Company, Boston.

THE SAME. 1883.

See under Collection of Novels and Tales by Henry James.

THE SAME. 1907.

See under Novels and Tales of Henry James, New York Edition.

THE SAME. 1920.

London: Thomas Nelson and Sons.

THE SAME. 1921.

See under Novels and Stories of Henry James, New and Complete Edition.

TRANSLATIONS

1876. Roderick Hudson. Roman von Henry James jun. Ins Deutsche übertragen von Moritz Busch.

Published in *Novellisten*, Amerikanische, Numbers 2 and 3. Leipzig: Grunow.

1884. Roderick Hudson, roman. Traduit de l'anglais par Léon Bochet.

Paris: Hachette et Cie.

1877

THE AMERICAN. / By / Henry James, Jr. / [publishers' device] / Boston: / James R. Osgood and Company, / Late Ticknor & Fields, and Fields, Osgood, & Co. / 1877.

12mo, pp. ii. 473, 5 blanks. Cloth.

Originally appeared in the *Atlantic Monthly*, June, 1876—May, 1877.

THE SAME. [1877] *First English Edition.*

London: Ward, Lock & Co.

THE SAME. 1878.

Published in *Collection of British Authors*, Volumes 1713 and 1714. Leipzig: Bernhard Tauchnitz.

THE SAME. 1879.

London: Macmillan and Co.

THE SAME. 1883.

See under Collection of Novels and Tales by Henry James.

THE SAME. 1907.

See under Novels and Tales of Henry James, New York Edition.

THE SAME. 1909.

London: T. Nelson and Sons.

THE SAME. 1921.

See under Novels and Stories of Henry James, New and Complete Edition.

TRANSLATIONS

1877. Der Amerikaner. Roman von Henry James jun. Ins Deutsche übertragen von Moritz Busch.

Published in *Novellisten*, Amerikanische, Numbers 6 and 7. Leipzig: Grunow.

1877. Der Amerikaner oder Marquis und Yankee. Roman von Henry James jun. Deutsch von Heichen-Abenheim.

Published in *Roman-Bibliothek transatlantische*, Numbers 4 and 5. Berlin: Abenheim.

1878. Der Amerikaner. Roman. Aus dem Amerikan.

Berlin: Janke.

1879. Amerykanin. Powiesc, Przeklad z Angielskiego a Callier.

Two volumes. Lemberg: Gūbryonowicz and Schmidt.

1884. L'Américain à Paris, roman. Traduit de l'anglais par Léon Bochet.

Two volumes. Paris: Hachette et Cie.

For an unpublished dramatization of *The American, see under* Unpublished Dramatic Works.

1878

WATCH AND WARD. / By / Henry James Jr. / [ornamental line] / Boston: / Houghton, Osgood and Company. / The Riverside Press, Cambridge. / 1878.

18mo, pp. ii. 219, 3 blanks. Cloth.

Originally appeared in the *Atlantic Monthly*, August–December, 1871.

The plates of the first edition of *Watch and Ward* were used (1886) in printing Number 6 in the Riverside Pocket Series, Boston: Houghton, Mifflin and Company.

For the reprinting of *Watch and Ward* in a collective volume, *see* the Index.

FRENCH / POETS AND NOVELISTS. / By / Henry James Jr. / London: / Macmillan and Co. / 1878. / [The right of translation and reproduction is reserved]

Crown 8vo, pp. viii. 440. Cloth.

Contents

Alfred de Musset.
Originally appeared in the *Galaxy*, June, 1877.

Théophile Gautier.
Originally appeared as a review of "Théâtre de Théophile Gautier: Mystères, Comédies, et Ballets." Paris: 1872, in the *North American Review*, April, 1873.

Charles Baudelaire.
Originally appeared in the *Nation*, April 27, 1876.

Honoré de Balzac.
Originally appeared in the *Galaxy*, December, 1875.

Balzac's Letters.
Originally appeared as a review of "The Letters of Honoré de Balzac" in the *Galaxy*, February, 1877.

George Sand.
Originally appeared in the *Galaxy*, July, 1877.

Charles de Bernard and Gustave Flaubert.
Originally appeared, under the title "The Minor French Novelists," in the *Galaxy*, February, 1876. This paper also included a consideration of the work of the Brothers de Goncourt, which has not been reprinted.

Ivan Turgénieff.
Originally appeared as a review of "Frühlingsfluthen. Ein König Lear des Dorfes. Zwei Novellen. Von Iwan Turgéniew." Mitau: 1873, in the *North American Review*, April, 1874.

The Two Ampères.
Originally appeared in the *Galaxy*, November, 1875.

Madame de Sabran.
Originally appeared, under the title "The Letters of Madame de Sabran," in the *Galaxy*, October, 1875.

Mérimée's Letters.
Originally appeared, under the title "The Letters of Prosper Mérimée," in the *Independent*, April 9, 1874.

The Théâtre Français.
Originally appeared in the *Galaxy*, April, 1877.

THE SAME. 1883.

Published in *Collection of British Authors*, Volume 2181. Leipzig: Bernhard Tauchnitz.

THE SAME. 1884.

London: Macmillan and Co.

THE EUROPEANS. / A Sketch. / By / Henry James, Jr. / In Two Volumes. / Vol. I. [II] / London: / Macmillan and Co. / 1878.
Crown 8vo. Vol. I. pp. iv. 255, 1 blank, fol-

lowed by publishers' advertisements, pp. 40. Vol.
II. pp. iv. 272. Cloth.

Originally appeared in the *Atlantic Monthly*, July–
October, 1878.

THE SAME. *First American Edition.*

THE EUROPEANS. / A Sketch. / By /
Henry James, Jr. / [publishers' device] / Bos-
ton: / Houghton, Osgood and Company. / The
Riverside Press, Cambridge. / 1879. [1878]

12mo, pp. vi. 281, 5 blanks. Cloth.

THE SAME. 1878.

Published in *Collection of British Authors*, Volume
1792. Leipzig: Bernhard Tauchnitz.

THE SAME. 1879.

London: Macmillan and Co.

THE SAME. 1883.

See under Collection of Novels and Tales by Henry
James.

THE SAME. 1921.

See under Novels and Stories of Henry James, New
and Complete Edition.

EUGEN PICKERING. Von Henry James.
Deutsch von Wilhelm Lange.

Published in *Universal-Bibliothek*, Number 1058.
Leipzig: Philipp Reclam jun. [1878]

A translation into German of "Eugene Pickering." For the original appearance of this tale and the first reprinting in a book, *see under* A Passionate Pilgrim and Other Tales.

1879

DAISY MILLER / A Study / By Henry James, Jr. / [line] / New York / Harper & Brothers, Publishers / Franklin Square / 1879. [1878]

32mo, pp. 116, 12 advts. Flexible cloth or wrappers. Published in *Harper's Half-Hour Series*, Number 82.

Originally appeared in the *Cornhill Magazine*, June–July, 1878.

THE SAME. 1901.

New York and London: Harper & Brothers.
The plates for this issue were made in 1892 for the edition of *Daisy Miller* and *An International Episode*, illustrated from drawings by Harry W. McVickar. In 1917 the same publishers reissued *Daisy Miller*, with an Introduction by W. D. Howells, using the same plates.

THE SAME. 1915.

See under Uniform Edition of the Tales of Henry James.

For reprintings of this tale in collective volumes, *see* the Index.

AN INTERNATIONAL EPISODE / By Henry James, Jr. / Author of "Daisy Miller" etc. / [line] / New York / Harper & Brothers, Publishers / Franklin Square / 1879. [1878]

32mo, pp. 136, 8 advts. Flexible cloth or wrappers. Published in *Harper's Half-Hour Series*, Number 91.

Originally appeared in the *Cornhill Magazine*, December, 1878—January, 1879.

The Same. 1902.

New York and London: Harper & Brothers.

The plates for this issue were made in 1892 for the edition of *Daisy Miller* and *An International Episode*, illustrated from drawings by Harry W. McVickar.

For reprintings of this tale in collective volumes, *see* the Index.

DAISY MILLER: A STUDY. / AN INTERNATIONAL EPISODE. / FOUR MEETINGS. / By Henry James, Jr. / In Two Volumes. / Vol. I. [II] / London: / Macmillan and Co. / 1879. / (Right of translation is reserved)

Crown 8vo. Vol. I. pp. viii. 271, 1 blank. Vol. II. pp. viii. 264. Cloth.

Contents. Volume I

Daisy Miller.

For original appearance and first reprinting in a book *see under* Daisy Miller. A Study.

An International Episode.

For original appearance and first reprinting in a book *see under* An International Episode.

Contents. Volume II

An International Episode, *continued.*

Four Meetings.
Originally appeared in *Scribner's Monthly*, November, 1877.

THE SAME. 1879.

Published in *Collection of British Authors*, Volume 1819. Leipzig: Bernhard Tauchnitz.

THE SAME. 1879.

London: Macmillan and Co.

THE SAME. 1918.

London: Thomas Nelson and Sons.

For reprintings of these tales in other collective volumes, *see* the Index.

TRANSLATIONS

1886. Daisy Miller, suivi de: Un Épisode international; Quatre rencontres: trois nouvelles. Traduites de l'anglais par Mme F. Pillon.

Paris: Fischbacher.

1920. Daisy Miller: En Studie. [En International Episode. Fire Moder.] Autoriseret oversættelse for Norge og Danmark af Ellen Christensen.

Kobenhavn & Kristiania: Martins Forlag.

HAWTHORNE / By / Henry James, Junr. / London / Macmillan and Co / 1879 / The

Right of Translation and Reproduction is Reserved.

Crown 8vo, pp. viii. 184, followed by publishers' advertisements, pp. 4. Cloth. Published in *English Men of Letters*, Edited by John Morley.

The earlier impressions of the English Edition of *Hawthorne* are without the Index, which is included in later issues.

THE SAME. *First American Edition.*

HAWTHORNE / By / Henry James, Jr. / [publishers' device] / New York / Harper & Brothers, Publishers / Franklin Square / 1880. [1879]

12mo, pp. [ii], viii. 177, 1 blank, 6 advts., 2 blanks. Cloth.

THE / MADONNA OF THE FUTURE / and Other Tales. / By / Henry James, Jr. / In Two Volumes. / Vol. I. [II] / London: / Macmillan and Co. / 1879. / The Right of Translation is Reserved.

Crown 8vo. Vol. I. pp. viii. 288. Vol. II. pp. viii. 246, 2 advts. Cloth.

Contents. Volume I

The Madonna of the Future.
For original appearance and first reprinting in a book, *see under* A Passionate Pilgrim and Other Tales.

Longstaff's Marriage.
Originally appeared in *Scribner's Monthly*, August, 1878.

Madame de Mauves.
> For original appearance and first reprinting in a book, *see under* A Passionate Pilgrim and Other Tales.

Contents. Volume II

Eugene Pickering.
> For original appearance and first reprinting in a book, *see under* A Passionate Pilgrim and Other Tales.

The Diary of a Man of Fifty.
> Originally appeared, simultaneously, in *Harper's Magazine* and *Macmillan's Magazine*, July, 1879.

Benvolio.
> Originally appeared in the *Galaxy*, August, 1875.

THE SAME. 1880.

Published in *Collection of British Authors*, Volumes 1881 and 1888. Leipzig: Bernhard Tauchnitz.

The contents of the earlier volume is the same as that of Volume I of the first edition of *The Madonna of the Future and Other Tales*. The contents of the later volume is the same as that of Volume II of the first edition of *The Madonna of the Future and Other Tales*.

THE SAME. 1880.

London: Macmillan and Co.

> For reprintings of these tales in other collective volumes, *see* the Index.

1880

THE / DIARY OF A MAN OF FIFTY / and / A BUNDLE OF LETTERS / By / Henry James, Jr. / Author of / "Daisy Miller" "An International Episode" etc. / [line] / New

York / Harper & Brothers, Publishers / Franklin Square / 1880.

32mo, pp. 135, 1 blank, 8 advts. Flexible cloth or wrappers. Published in *Harper's Half-Hour Series*, Number 135.

Contents

The Diary of a Man of Fifty.
> For original appearance and first reprinting in a book, *see under* The Madonna of the Future and Other Tales.

A Bundle of Letters.
> Originally appeared in the *Parisian*, December 18, 1879.
>
> For reprintings of these tales in other collective volumes, *see* the Index.

A BUNDLE OF LETTERS. (Reprinted from the *Parisian*.)

Square 12mo. Boston: Loring. Wrappers. [1880]

For original appearance and first reprinting in a book, *see under* The Diary of a Man of Fifty and A Bundle of Letters.

A BUNDLE OF LETTERS. (Preceded by *Sweet Nelly*, *My Heart's Delight*. By Walter Besant and James Rice.)

Published in *Seaside Library*, Number 702. New York: George Munro. 1880.

For original appearance and first reprinting in a book, *see under* The Diary of a Man of Fifty and A Bundle of Letters.

CONFIDENCE. / By Henry James, Jr. / [publishers' device] / Boston: / Houghton, Osgood and Company. / The Riverside Press, Cambridge. / 1880.

12mo, pp. ii. 347, 3 blanks. Cloth.

Originally appeared in *Scribner's Monthly*, August, 1879—January, 1880.

THE SAME. *First English Edition.*

CONFIDENCE / By Henry James Jr. / [publishers' device] / In Two Volumes / Vol. I. [II] / London / Chatto & Windus, Piccadilly / 1880 / All rights reserved.

Crown 8vo. Vol. I. pp. iv. 309, 1 blank, 1 publishers' mark, 1 blank. Vol. II. pp. iv. 253, 1 blank, 1 publishers' mark, 1 blank, followed by publishers' advertisements, pp. 32. Cloth.

THE SAME. 1880.

Published in *Collection of British Authors*, Volume 1901. Leipzig: Bernhard Tauchnitz.

THE SAME. 1880.

London: Chatto & Windus.

THE SAME. 1883.

See under Collection of Novels and Tales by Henry James.

THE SAME. 1921.

See under Novels and Stories of Henry James, New and Complete Edition.

1881

WASHINGTON SQUARE / By Henry James, Jr. / Author of / "Daisy Miller" "An International Episode" Etc. / Illustrated by George Du Maurier / New York / Harper & Brothers, Franklin Square / 1881. [1880]

16mo, pp. ii. 266, 6 advts., 2 blanks. Cloth.

Originally appeared in the *Cornhill Magazine*, June–November, and in *Harper's Magazine*, July–December, 1880.

In 1926 an issue from these plates appeared in the *American Library*. New York: Albert & Charles Boni.

THE SAME. 1883.

See under Collection of Novels and Tales by Henry James.

THE SAME. 1921.

See under Novels and Stories of Henry James, New and Complete Edition.

For reprintings of *Washington Square* in collective volumes, *see* the Index.

WASHINGTON SQUARE / THE PENSION BEAUREPAS / A BUNDLE OF LETTERS / By Henry James, Jun. / Vol. I. [II] / London / Macmillan and Co. / 1881.

Crown 8vo. Vol. I. pp. viii. 265, 3 blanks. Vol. II. pp. iv. 371, 1 blank. Cloth.

Contents. Volume I

Washington Square.

For original appearance and first reprinting in a book, *see under* Washington Square.

Contents. Volume II

Washington Square, *continued.*

The Pension Beaurepas.
Originally appeared in the *Atlantic Monthly*, April, 1879.

A Bundle of Letters.
For original appearance and first reprinting in a book, *see
under* The Diary of a Man of Fifty and A Bundle of Letters.

THE SAME. 1881.

Published in *Collection of British Authors*, Volumes
1977 and 1978. Leipzig: Bernhard Tauchnitz.

THE SAME. 1881.

London: Macmillan and Co.

For reprintings of these stories in other collective volumes,
see the Index.

THE PORTRAIT OF A LADY / By /
Henry James, Jr., / Author of "The Europeans," Etc., Etc. / In Three Volumes. / Vol. I.
[II] [III] / London: / Macmillan and Co. /
1881. / The Right of Translation and Reproduction is Reserved.

Crown 8vo. Vol. I. pp. iv. 266, 2 blanks. Vol.
II. pp. iv. 254, 2 blanks. Vol. III. pp. iv. 248,
followed by publishers' advertisements, pp. 24.
Cloth.

Originally appeared in *Macmillan's Magazine*, October, 1880—November, 1881; and in the *Atlantic
Monthly*, November, 1880—December, 1881.

THE SAME. *First American Edition.*

THE / PORTRAIT OF A LADY. / By / Henry James, Jr. / [publishers' device] / Boston: / Houghton, Mifflin and Company. / New York: 11 East Seventeenth Street. / The Riverside Press, Cambridge. / 1882. [1881]

12mo, pp. iv. 520, 4 blanks. Cloth.

THE SAME. 1882.

Published in *Collection of British Authors*, Volumes 2042, 2043, 2044. Leipzig: Bernhard Tauchnitz.

THE SAME. 1882.

London: Macmillan and Co.

THE SAME. 1883.

See under Collection of Novels and Tales by Henry James.

THE SAME. 1908.

See under Novels and Tales of Henry James, New York Edition.

THE SAME. 1921.

See under Novels and Stories of Henry James, New and Complete Edition.

1883

FOREIGN PARTS.

Published in *Collection of British Authors*, Volume 2164. Leipzig: Bernhard Tauchnitz.

Note on p. 5. "The papers in this volume, reprinted from periodicals, were collected and published in Boston in the year 1875, under the name of *Transatlantic Sketches*. For this 'Tauchnitz Edition' the name has been changed and the sketches have been revised."

The contents of *Foreign Parts* is the same as that of *Transatlantic Sketches*, except for the omission of four complete papers, and parts of another, included in the previous volume. For these omissions *see under* Transatlantic Sketches.

DAISY MILLER—A Study—And Other Stories.

Published in *Franklin Square Library*, Number 303. New York: Harper & Brothers, 1883.

Contents

Daisy Miller.
> For original appearance and first reprinting in a book, *see under* Daisy Miller. A Study.

An International Episode.
> For original appearance and first reprinting in a book, *see under* An International Episode.

The Diary of a Man of Fifty.
> For original appearance and first reprinting in a book, *see under* The Diary of a Man of Fifty and A Bundle of Letters.

A Bundle of Letters.
> For original appearance and first reprinting in a book, *see under* The Diary of a Man of Fifty and A Bundle of Letters.

> This is the single instance in which these four short stories have been assembled to make the contents of a separate book. For reprintings of these tales in other collective volumes, *see* the Index.

THE SIEGE OF LONDON, / THE PENSION BEAUREPAS, / and / THE POINT OF VIEW. / By / Henry James, Jr. / Author of "Daisy Miller," "The American," / "The Portrait of a Lady," Etc. / [publishers' device] / Boston: / James R. Osgood and Company. / 1883.

12mo, pp. vi. 294. Cloth.

Contents

The Siege of London.

> Originally appeared in the *Cornhill Magazine*, January–February, 1883.

The Pension Beaurepas.

> For original appearance and first reprinting in a book, *see under* Washington Square and Other Tales.

The Point of View.

> Originally appeared in the *Century Magazine*, December, 1882.

> For a translation of *The Siege of London* into French ("La Conquête de Londres") as a contribution to a periodical, *see* the Index.

> For reprintings of these tales in other collective volumes, *see* the Index.

> After the death of his father, Henry James, Sr., Henry James omitted the "Jr.," which had previously appeared with his name on the title-pages of his books. It is probable that the title-page described above was the last to be printed before the change.

PORTRAITS OF PLACES / By / Henry James / London / Macmillan and Co. / 1883.

Crown 8vo, pp. viii. 376. Cloth.

Contents

I. Venice.

> Originally appeared in the *Century Magazine*, November, 1882.

II. Italy Revisited.
Originally appeared in the *Atlantic Monthly*, April, 1878.

III. Occasional Paris.
Originally appeared, under the title "Paris Revisited," in the *Galaxy*, January, 1878.

IV. Rheims and Laon: A Little Tour.
Originally appeared, under the title "A Little Tour in France," in the *Atlantic Monthly*, January, 1878.

V. Chartres.
Originally appeared, under the title "Chartres Portrayed," in the *New York Tribune*, April 29, 1876.

VI. Rouen.
Originally appeared, under the title "Summer in France," in the *New York Tribune*, August 12, 1876.

VII. Etretat.
Originally appeared, under the title "A French Watering Place," in the *New York Tribune*, August 26, 1876.

VIII. From Normandy to the Pyrenees.
Originally appeared in the *Galaxy*, January, 1877.

IX. An English Easter.
Originally appeared in *Lippincott's Magazine*, July, 1877.

X. London at Midsummer.
Originally appeared in *Lippincott's Magazine*, November, 1877.

XI. Two Excursions.
Originally appeared, as part of an article, under the title "Three Excursions," in the *Galaxy*, September, 1877.

XII. In Warwickshire.
Originally appeared in the *Galaxy*, November, 1877.

XIII. Abbeys and Castles.
Originally appeared in *Lippincott's Magazine*, October, 1877.

XIV. English Vignettes.
Originally appeared in *Lippincott's Magazine*, April, 1879.

XV. An English New Year.
Originally appeared in the *Nation*, January 23, 1879.

XVI. An English Winter Watering-Place.
Originally appeared in the *Nation*, April 3, 1879.

XVII. Saratoga.
Originally appeared in the *Nation*, August 11, 1870.

XVIII. Newport.
Originally appeared in the *Nation*, September 15, 1870.

XIX. Quebec.
Originally appeared in the *Nation*, September 28–October 5, 1871.

XX. Niagara.
Originally appeared in the *Nation*, October 12–19, 1871.

THE SAME. *First American Edition.*

Henry James / [line] / PORTRAITS OF PLACES / [publishers' device] / Boston / James R. Osgood and Company / [line] / 1884. [1883]

12mo, pp. viii. 376. Cloth.

The only variations between the plates of the first English and first American Editions of *Portraits of Places* are in the front matter, pages i–vi, where, beside the differences in the title-pages, shown above, the introductory notes are not the same.

THE SAME. 1884.

Published in *Collection of British Authors*, Volume 2276. Leipzig: Bernhard Tauchnitz.

For reprintings of these papers in collective volumes, *see* the Index.

Henry James / [line] / DAISY MILLER / A Comedy / In Three Acts / [publishers' device] / Boston / James R. Osgood and Company / [line] / 1883.

12mo, pp. ii. 189, 1 blank. Cloth.

This is the first published edition, in book form, of a comedy based on the author's "Study," *Daisy Miller*. It originally appeared in the *Atlantic Monthly*, April–June, 1883.

For an unpublished stage version of *Daisy Miller, see under* Unpublished Dramatic Works.

1884

NOTES / (No. 15 of Series) / By / Mr. Henry James / on a / COLLECTION OF DRAWINGS / By / MR. GEORGE DU-MAURIER / Exhibited / at / The Fine Art Society's / 148 New Bond Street / 1884.

8 x 5¼ inches, pp. 66 (including a frontispiece from an unpublished drawing by George Du Maurier). Wrappers.

The Notes by Henry James include pp. 5–17.

THE SIEGE OF LONDON. THE POINT OF VIEW. A PASSIONATE PILGRIM.

Published in *Collection of British Authors*, Volume 2234. Leipzig: Bernhard Tauchnitz.

This is the single instance in which these three short stories have been assembled to make the contents of a separate book.

For the original appearances and reprintings of these tales in other collective volumes, *see* the Index.

Henry James / [line] / TALES OF THREE CITIES / [publishers' device] / Boston / James R. Osgood and Company / [line] / 1884.
   12mo, pp. iv. 359, 1 blank. Cloth.

Contents

The Impressions of a Cousin.
> Originally appeared in the *Century Magazine*, November–December, 1883.

Lady Barberina.
> Originally appeared in the *Century Magazine*, May–July, 1884.

A New England Winter.
> Originally appeared in the *Century Magazine*, August–September, 1884.

THE SAME. *First English Edition.*

TALES / OF / THREE CITIES / By / Henry James / London / Macmillan and Co. / 1884.
   Crown 8vo, pp. viii. 309, 1 blank, 2 advts. Cloth.

The order of sequence of the stories varies in the American and English Editions. That of the American Edition is given above. The sequence in the English Edition is,—Lady Barberina—A New England Winter—The Impressions of a Cousin.

> For reprintings of these tales in other collective volumes, *see* the Index.

1885

Henry James / [line] / A LITTLE TOUR IN FRANCE / [publishers' device] / Boston

/ James R. Osgood and Company / [line] / 1885. [1884]

12mo, pp. iv. 255, 1 blank. Cloth.

Originally appeared, under the title "En Provence," in the *Atlantic Monthly*, July–November, 1883, and February, April, and May, 1884.

THE SAME. 1885.

Published in *Collection of British Authors*, Volume 2334. Leipzig: Bernhard Tauchnitz.

THE SAME. 1900.

London: William Heinemann.
This edition includes ninety-four illustrations by Joseph Pennell and for it the author wrote a new Preface.

THE SAME. 1900.

Boston and New York: Houghton, Mifflin and Company.
This is the American Edition with illustrations by Joseph Pennell and the author's new Preface. A large paper issue of the American Edition was limited to two hundred and fifty copies.

STORIES REVIVED / In Three Volumes / Vol. I. / THE AUTHOR OF 'BELTRAFFIO.' PANDORA. / THE PATH OF DUTY. / A DAY OF DAYS. A LIGHT MAN. / By / Henry James / London / Macmillan and Co. / 1885.

Crown 8vo, pp. viii. 280. Cloth.

Contents

The Author of *Beltraffio*.
> Originally appeared in the *English Illustrated Magazine*, June–July, 1884.

Pandora.
> In his Preface to Vol. XVIII of the New York Edition of his *Novels and Tales*, in which this tale is included, Henry James states that it was "first given to the light in a New York newspaper in 1884." The name of the newspaper and the date of the original appearance are not established.

The Path of Duty.
> Originally appeared in the *English Illustrated Magazine*, December, 1884.

A Light Man.
> For original appearance and first reprinting in a book, *see under* Stories by American Authors, Vol. V.

A Day of Days.
> Originally appeared in the *Galaxy*, June 15, 1866.
> The sequence of the last two tales has been transposed from that shown on the title-page to that shown in the Contents.

STORIES REVIVED / In Three Volumes / Vol. II. / GEORGINA'S REASONS. A PASSIONATE / PILGRIM. A LAND-SCAPE-PAINTER. / ROSE-AGATHE. / By / Henry James / London / Macmillan and Co. / 1885.
Crown 8vo, pp. viii. 280. Cloth.

Contents

Georgina's Reasons.
> No previous appearance of this story has been established.

A Passionate Pilgrim.
> For original appearance and first reprinting in a book, *see under* A Passionate Pilgrim and Other Tales.

A Landscape-Painter.
   Originally appeared in the *Atlantic Monthly*, February, 1866.
Rose-Agathe.
   Originally appeared, under the title "Théodolinde," in *Lippincott's Magazine*, May, 1878.

STORIES REVIVED / In Three Volumes / Vol. III. / POOR RICHARD. THE LAST OF THE VALERII. / MASTER EUSTACE. / THE ROMANCE OF CERTAIN OLD CLOTHES. / A MOST EXTRAORDINARY CASE. / By / Henry James / London / Macmillan and Co. / 1885.
   Crown 8vo, pp. viii. 269, 1 blank, 2 advts. Cloth.

Contents

Poor Richard.
   Originally appeared in the *Atlantic Monthly*, June–August, 1867.
The Last of the Valerii.
   For original appearance and first reprinting in a book, *see under* A Passionate Pilgrim and Other Tales.
Master Eustace.
   Originally appeared in the *Galaxy*, November, 1871.
The Romance of Certain Old Clothes.
   For original appearance and first reprinting in a book, *see under* A Passionate Pilgrim and Other Tales.
A Most Extraordinary Case.
   Originally appeared in the *Atlantic Monthly*, April, 1868.

THE SAME. Two Volumes. 1885.
   London: Macmillan and Co.
   For reprintings of these tales in other collective volumes, *see* the Index.

Henry James / [line] / THE AUTHOR OF
BELTRAFFIO / PANDORA [ornament]
GEORGINA'S REASONS / THE PATH
OF DUTY / FOUR MEETINGS / [pub-
lishers' device] / Boston / James R. Osgood and
Company / [line] / 1885.
  12mo, pp. ii. 362. Cloth.

None of the tales in this group had previously appeared in a collective volume in America. For the original
appearance and first reprinting in a book of The Author
of Beltraffio, Pandora, and The Path of Duty, *see under*
Stories Revived, Vol. I. For the original appearance and
first reprinting in a book of Georgina's Reasons, *see under* Stories Revived, Vol. II. For the original appearance
and first reprinting in a book of Four Meetings, *see under*
Daisy Miller and Other Tales, Vol. II.

> For reprintings of these tales in other collective volumes, *see*
> the Index.

1886

THE / BOSTONIANS / A Novel / By /
Henry James / In Three Volumes / Vol. I. [II]
[III] / London / Macmillan and Co. / 1886.
  Crown 8vo. Vol. I. pp. iv. 244. Vol. II. pp. iv.
226, 2 advts. Vol. III. pp. iv. 232, 4 advts.
Cloth.

Originally appeared in the *Century Magazine*, February, 1885—February, 1886.

THE SAME. 1886.

London and New York: Macmillan and Co.

THE SAME. 1921.

See under Novels and Stories of Henry James, New and Complete Edition.

THE / PRINCESS CASAMASSIMA / A

Novel / By / Henry James / In Three Volumes / Vol. I. [II] [III] / London / Macmillan and Co. / and New York / 1886.

Crown 8vo. Vol. I. pp. iv. 252. Vol. II. pp. iv. 257, 1 blank, 2 advts. Vol. III. pp. iv. 242, 2 advts. Cloth.

Originally appeared in the *Atlantic Monthly*, September, 1885—October, 1886.

THE SAME. 1886.

London and New York: Macmillan and Co.

THE SAME. 1908.

See under Novels and Tales of Henry James, New York Edition.

THE SAME. 1921.

See under Novels and Stories of Henry James, New and Complete Edition.

1888

PARTIAL PORTRAITS / By / Henry

James / London / Macmillan and Co. / and New York / 1888 / All Rights Reserved.

Globe 8vo, pp. xii. 408, 4 advts. Cloth.

34 ORIGINAL WORKS [1888

Contents

I. Emerson.
Originally appeared, under the title "The Life of Emerson," in *Macmillan's Magazine*, December, 1887.

II. The Life of George Eliot.
Originally appeared, under the title "George Eliot's Life," in the *Atlantic Monthly*, May, 1885.

III. Daniel Deronda: A Conversation.
Originally appeared in the *Atlantic Monthly*, December, 1876.

IV. Anthony Trollope.
Originally appeared in the *Century Magazine*, July, 1883.

V. Robert Louis Stevenson.
Originally appeared in the *Century Magazine*, April, 1888.

VI. Miss Woolson.
Originally appeared, under the title "Miss Constance Fenimore Woolson," in *Harper's Weekly*, February 12, 1887.

VII. Alphonse Daudet.
Originally appeared in the *Century Magazine*, August, 1883.

VIII. Guy de Maupassant.
Originally appeared in the *Fortnightly Review*, March, 1888.

IX. Ivan Turgénieff.
Originally appeared in the *Atlantic Monthly*, January, 1884. For a later reprinting of this paper in a book, *see under* The Novels and Stories of Ivan Turgénieff.

X. George du Maurier.
Originally appeared, under the title "Du Maurier and London Society," in the *Century Magazine*, May, 1883.

XI. The Art of Fiction.
For original appearance and first reprinting in a book, *see under* The Art of Fiction.

THE ASPERN PAPERS / LOUISA PALLANT / THE MODERN WARNING / By / Henry James / In Two Volumes—

Vol. I [II] / London / Macmillan and Co. / and New York / 1888 / All Rights Reserved.

Globe 8vo. Vol. I. pp. viii. 239, 1 blank. Vol. II. pp. viii. 258, 6 advts. Cloth.

Contents. Volume I

The Aspern Papers.
> Originally appeared in the *Atlantic Monthly*, March–May, 1888.

Contents. Volume II

Louisa Pallant.
> Originally appeared in *Harper's Magazine*, February, 1888.

The Modern Warning.
> Originally appeared, under the title "Two Countries," in *Harper's Magazine*, June, 1888.

THE SAME. 1888.

> London and New York: Macmillan and Co.

> For reprintings of the *Aspern Papers* as a separate book, *see* the Index.
> For a translation of the *Aspern Papers* into French ("Les Papiers de Jeffroy Aspern") as a contribution to a periodical, *see* the Index.
> For reprintings of these tales in other collective volumes, *see* the Index.

THE / REVERBERATOR / By / Henry James / In Two Volumes / Vol. I. [II] / London / Macmillan and Co. / and New York / 1888 / All Rights Reserved.

Globe 8vo. Vol. I. pp. iv. 190, 2 advts. Vol. II. pp. iv. 208. Cloth.

Originally appeared in *Macmillan's Magazine*, February–July, 1888.

THE SAME. 1888.

London and New York: Macmillan and Co.

THE SAME. 1916.

See under Uniform Edition of the Tales of Henry James.

For reprintings of *The Reverberator* in collective volumes, *see* the Index.

1889

A LONDON LIFE / THE PATAGONIA / THE LIAR / MRS. TEMPERLEY / By / Henry James / In Two Volumes—Vol. I [II] / London / Macmillan and Co. / and New York / 1889 / All rights reserved.

Globe 8vo. Vol. I. pp. viii. 281, 1 blank, 2 advts. Vol. II. pp. viii. 361, 1 blank, 2 advts. Cloth.

Contents. Volume I

A London Life.

Originally appeared in *Scribner's Magazine*, June–September, 1888.

Contents. Volume II

The Patagonia.

Originally appeared in the *English Illustrated Magazine*, August–September, 1888.

The Liar.

Originally appeared in the *Century Magazine*, May–June, 1888.

Mrs. Temperley.

Originally appeared, under the title "Cousin Maria," in *Harper's Weekly*, August 6, 13, and 20, 1887.

THE SAME. 1889.

London and New York: Macmillan and Co.

THE SAME. 1891.

Published in the *English Library*, Volume 30. Leipzig: Heinemann and Balestier.

For reprintings of these tales in other collective volumes, *see* the Index.

1890

THE TRAGIC MUSE / By / Henry James / In Two Volumes / Vol. I. [II] / [publishers' device] / Boston and New York / Houghton, Mifflin and Company / The Riverside Press, Cambridge / 1890.

16mo. Vol. I. pp. vi. 1–422, 2 blanks. Vol. II. pp. iv. 423–882, 2 blanks. Cloth.

Originally appeared in the *Atlantic Monthly*, January, 1889—May, 1890.

THE SAME. *First English Edition.*

THE TRAGIC MUSE / By / Henry James / In Three Volumes / Vol. I. [II] [III] / London / Macmillan and Co. / and New York / 1890 / The Right of Translation and Reproduction is Reserved.

Globe 8vo. Vol. I. pp. iv. 248. Vol. II. pp. iv. 252. Vol. III. pp. iv. 258, 2 blanks. Cloth.

THE SAME. 1891.

London and New York: Macmillan and Co.

THE SAME. 1908.

See under Novels and Tales of Henry James, New York Edition.

THE SAME. 1920.

London: Thomas Nelson and Sons.

THE SAME. 1921.

See under Novels and Stories of Henry James, New and Complete Edition.

1891

CATALOGUE / OF A / COLLECTION OF DRAWINGS / By / ALFRED PAR- SONS, R. I. / With a Prefatory Note / By / Henry James. / Exhibited at / The Fine Art Society's. / 148, New Bond Street, W., / Lon- don / 1891.

8 x 5¼ inches, pp. 15, 1 blank. [Page 1 serves as title-page] No cover.

The Prefatory Note by Henry James, pp. 3–11, is re- printed in *Picture and Text*, under the title, "Alfred Parsons."

1892

THE LESSON OF THE MASTER / THE MARRIAGES THE PUPIL / BROOKSMITH / THE SOLUTION SIR EDMUND ORME / By / Henry James /

New York / Macmillan and Co. / and London / 1892 / All rights reserved.
   12mo, pp. vi. 302, 12 advts. Cloth.

Contents

The Lesson of the Master.
   Originally appeared in the *Universal Review*, July 16–August 15, 1888.

The Marriages.
   Originally appeared in the *Atlantic Monthly*, August, 1891.

The Pupil.
   Originally appeared in *Longman's Magazine*, March–April, 1891.

Brooksmith.
   Originally appeared in *Harper's Weekly*, May 2, 1891.

The Solution.
   Originally appeared in the *New Review*, December, 1889—February, 1890.

Sir Edmund Orme.
   In his Preface to Volume XVII of the New York Edition of his *Novels and Tales*, in which this tale is included, Henry James "presumes" that Sir Edmund Orme "must first have appeared in a weekly newspaper." The name of the newspaper and the date of the original appearance are not established.

THE SAME. *First English Edition.*

THE LESSON OF THE MASTER / THE MARRIAGES THE PUPIL / BROOKSMITH / THE SOLUTION SIR EDMUND ORME / By / Henry James / London / Macmillan and Co. / and New York / 1892 / All rights reserved.
   Crown 8vo, pp. [ii], vi. 302, 2 blanks, fol-

lowed by publishers' advertisements, pp. 48. Cloth.

The plates of the first American Edition were used in printing the first English Edition, the only variations being in the title-pages and the advertisements.

THE SAME. 1892.

Published in the *English Library*, Volume 135. Leipzig: Heinemann and Balestier.

> For reprintings of *The Lesson of the Master* and *The Pupil* as separate books, *see* the Index.
> For a translation of *The Pupil* into French ("L'Élève") as a contribution to a periodical, *see* the Index.
> For reprintings of these tales in other collective volumes, *see* the Index.

DAISY MILLER & AN INTERNATIONAL EPISODE. Illustrated from drawings by Harry W. McVickar. New York: Harper & Brothers.

For original appearance and first reprinting in a book of *Daisy Miller*, *see under* Daisy Miller: A Study.

For original appearance and first reprinting in a book of *An International Episode*, *see under* An International Episode.

An edition de luxe of this illustrated edition of *Daisy Miller* and *An International Episode*, limited to two hundred and fifty copies, was also issued in 1892.

The plates of this illustrated edition of *Daisy Miller* and *An International Episode* were later used, with the imprint of Harper & Brothers, New York, for printing separate issues of both stories:—Daisy Miller, 1901; An International Episode, 1902. Another issue of *Daisy Miller* from the same plates, and with the same imprint, with an Introduction by W. D. Howells, was published in 1917. In 1918 a new set of plates, including the Introduction by W. D. Howells, was used in reprinting *Daisy Miller* and *An International Episode* with the imprint of Boni & Liveright, New York, in the format of their Modern Library of the World's Best Books.

THE SAME. 1927.

New York: The Macmillan Co. Introduction by Martin W. Sampson. No illustrations. Published in *Modern Readers' Series*.

For reprintings of these tales in other collective volumes, *see* the Index.

1893

THE PRIVATE LIFE / LORD BEAU-PRÉ / THE VISITS / By / Henry James / [publishers' device] / New York / Harper & Brothers Publishers / 1893.

16mo, pp. vi. 232, 4 advts. Cloth.

Contents

The Private Life.
Originally appeared in the *Atlantic Monthly*, April, 1892.

Lord Beaupré.
Originally appeared, under the title "Lord Beauprey," in *Macmillan's Magazine*, April–June, 1892.

The Visits.
This tale appears here for the first time.

These tales, together with The Wheel of Time, Collaboration, and Owen Wingrave, were assembled (1893) for publication in a single volume in England.
For reprintings of these tales in other collective volumes, *see* the Index.

THE WHEEL OF TIME / COLLABO-
RATION / OWEN WINGRAVE / By /
Henry James / [publishers' device] / New York
/ Harper & Brothers Publishers / 1893.
    16mo, pp. iv. 220. Cloth.

Contents

The Wheel of Time.
    Originally appeared in the *Cosmopolitan*, December, 1892—
    January, 1893.

Collaboration.
    Originally appeared in the *English Illustrated Magazine*,
    September, 1892.

Owen Wingrave.
    This tale appears here for the first time.
    For an unpublished dramatization of Owen Wingrave, under
    the title "The Saloon, A Play in One Act," *see under* Un-
    published Dramatic Works.

    These tales, together with The Private Life, Lord Beaupré,
    and The Visits were assembled (1893) for publication in a
    single volume in England.
    For reprintings of these tales in other collective volumes, *see*
    the Index.

THE PRIVATE LIFE / THE WHEEL
OF TIME LORD BEAUPRE / THE
VISITS COLLABORATION / OWEN
WINGRAVE / By / Henry James / London
/ James R. Osgood, McIlvaine & Co. / 45, Al-
bemarle Street, W. / 1893.
    Crown 8vo, pp. viii. 332. Cloth.

    These tales, which the American publishers issued in
two separate volumes (1893), were assembled for a single
volume, when they were first published in an English

Edition. For their original appearance and first reprinting in a book, *see under* The Private Life and Other Tales, American Edition, or The Wheel of Time and Other Tales.

For reprintings of these tales in other collective volumes, *see* the Index.

THE REAL THING / and Other Tales / By / Henry James / New York / Macmillan and Co. / and London / 1893 / All rights reserved.

12mo, pp. x. 275, 1 blank, 2 advts. Cloth.

Contents

The Real Thing.
This tale appears here for the first time.

Sir Dominick Ferrand.
Originally appeared, under the title "Jersey Villas," in the *Cosmopolitan*, July–August, 1892.

Nona Vincent.
Originally appeared in the *English Illustrated Magazine*, February–March, 1892.

The Chaperon.
Originally appeared in the *Atlantic Monthly*, November–December, 1891.

Greville Fane.
In his Preface to Volume XVI of the New York Edition of his *Novels and Tales*, in which this tale is included, Henry James indicates that Greville Fane first appeared "in a London weekly at the beginning of the nineties." The name of the weekly and the date of the original appearance are not established.

THE SAME. *First English Edition.*

THE REAL THING / and Other Tales / By / Henry James / London / Macmillan and

Co. / and New York / 1893 / All rights reserved.

Crown 8vo, pp. x. 275, 3 blanks, followed by publishers' advertisements, pp. 48. Cloth.

The plates of the first American Edition were used in printing the first English Edition, the only variations being in the title-pages and the advertisements.

For reprintings of these tales in other collective volumes, *see* the Index.

PICTURE [in red] / AND TEXT [in red] / By / Henry James / [publishers' device on a block in buff tint] / New York / Harper and Brothers [in red] / MDCCCXCIII.

16mo, pp. xii. 175, 1 blank. Portraits. Plates. Cloth. Published in *Harper's American Essayists.*

Contents

Black and White.
Originally appeared, under the title "Our Artists in Europe," in *Harper's Magazine*, June, 1889.

Edwin A. Abbey.
Originally appeared in *Harper's Weekly*, December 4, 1886.

Charles S. Reinhart.
Originally appeared in *Harper's Weekly*, June 14, 1890.

Alfred Parsons.
Originally appeared (1891) as a "Prefatory Note" in a catalogue of an exhibition of the artist's pictures.

John S. Sargent.
Originally appeared in *Harper's Magazine*, October, 1887.

Honoré Daumier.
Originally appeared, under the title "Daumier, Caricaturist," in the *Century Magazine*, January, 1890.

After the Play.
Originally appeared in the *New Review*, June, 1889.

ESSAYS IN LONDON / AND / ELSE-WHERE / By / Henry James / [publishers' device] / New York / Harper & Brothers Publishers / 1893.

12mo, pp. viii. 305, 1 blank, 6 advts. Cloth.

Contents

London.
Originally appeared in the *Century Magazine*, December, 1888.

James Russell Lowell.
Originally appeared in the *Atlantic Monthly*, January, 1892.

Frances Anne Kemble.
Originally appeared in *Temple Bar*, April, 1893.

Gustave Flaubert.
Originally appeared in *Macmillan's Magazine*, March, 1893.

Pierre Loti.
Originally appeared in the *Fortnightly Review*, May, 1888.

The Journal of the Brothers de Goncourt.
Originally appeared in the *Fortnightly Review*, October, 1888.

Browning in Westminster Abbey.
No previous appearance of this paper, dated 1890, has been recorded.

Henrik Ibsen.
I. On the occasion of "Hedda Gabler." Originally appeared in the *New Review*, June, 1891.
II. On the occasion of "The Master-Builder." No previous appearance of this paper, dated 1893, has been recorded.

Mrs. Humphry Ward.
Originally appeared in the *English Illustrated Magazine*, February, 1892.

Criticism.
>Originally appeared, under the title "The Science of Criticism," in the *New Review*, May, 1891.

An Animated Conversation.
>Originally appeared in *Scribner's Magazine*, March, 1889.

THE SAME. *First English Edition.*

ESSAYS IN LONDON / AND ELSE-
WHERE / By / Henry James / London /
James R. Osgood, McIlvaine & Co. / 45 Albemarle Street, W. / MDCCCXCIII / All rights reserved.
>Post 8vo, pp. viii. 320. Cloth.

1894

THEATRICALS / [line] / TWO COME-
DIES / TENANTS DISENGAGED / By
/ Henry James / London / Osgood, McIlvaine
& Co. / 45 Albemarle Street / 1894 / All rights
reserved.
>Post 8vo, pp. viii. 325, 1 blank, 1 advt., 1
blank. Cloth.

>Sheets of the English Edition were used for the American Edition. With the exception of the imprint of the American publishers—Harper & Brothers, New York—and the omission of the page of advertisements, the two editions are identical.

1895

"THE QUEST OF / THE HOLY
GRAIL." / The first portion of a Series of /

Paintings to be done for the / Decoration of the / Public Library of Boston, U. S. A. / By Edwin A. Abbey. / [line] / Now shown for a limited period / at the Galleries 9, Conduit St., W. / Daily from 10 a.m. to 6 p.m. / January 1895.

7¼ x 5 inches, pp. 7, 1 blank. [Page 1 serves as title-page] No cover.

This Summary of Scenes of the first portion of The Story of the Grail by Henry James was issued anonymously.

Mr. E. V. Lucas, in his *Record of the Life and Work of Edwin Austin Abbey* (1921), states that a Summary of the Scenes for The Story of the Grail, Second Part, exhibited at the Guildhall, London, in 1901, before they were brought to America, was the composite work of Mrs. Abbey and Henry James. A printed copy of this Summary has not been available for description in this record.

THEATRICALS / SECOND SERIES / THE ALBUM THE REPROBATE / By / Henry James / London / Osgood, McIlvaine & Co. / 45 Albemarle Street / 1895 / All rights reserved.

Post 8vo, pp. xvi. 416, followed by publishers' advertisements, pp. 2. Cloth.

Sheets of the English Edition were used for the American Edition. With the exception of the imprint of the American publishers—Harper & Brothers, New York— and the omission of advertising, the two editions are identical.

TERMINATIONS / THE DEATH OF THE LION / THE COXON FUND /

THE MIDDLE YEARS / THE ALTAR
OF THE DEAD / By / Henry James / Author of "Daisy Miller" Etc. / [publishers' de-
vice] / New York / Harper & Brothers Publishers / 1895.

12mo, pp. viii. 242, 6 advts. Cloth.

Contents

The Death of the Lion.
Originally appeared in the *Yellow Book*, April, 1894.
The Coxon Fund.
Originally appeared in the *Yellow Book*, July, 1894.
The Middle Years.
Originally appeared in *Scribner's Magazine*, May, 1893.
The Altar of the Dead.
This tale appears here for the first time.

THE SAME. *First English Edition.*

TERMINATIONS [in red] / THE
DEATH OF THE / LION . . THE
COXON / FUND . . THE MIDDLE /
YEARS . . THE ALTAR / OF THE
DEAD . . . . . / By Henry James / [orna-
ment] / London: William Heinemann [in red]
/ MDCCCXCV.

Crown 8vo, pp. viii. 260, followed by publishers' advertisements, pp. 16. Cloth.

For reprintings of *The Death of the Lion*, *The Coxon Fund*,
and *The Altar of the Dead* as separate books, *see* the Index.
For reprintings of these tales in other collective volumes, *see*
the Index.
For a translation of *The Altar of the Dead* into French
("L'Autel des Morts") as a contribution to a periodical, *see*

the Index. A translation, in book form, of this tale has also
been announced for early publication by Librairie Stock
(Delamain et Boutelleau), Paris.

1896

EMBARRASSMENTS / By / Henry James
/ Author of "Daisy Miller," "The Europeans"
/ Etc., Etc. / New York / The Macmillan
Company / London: Macmillan & Co., Ltd. /
1896 / All rights reserved.

12mo, pp. vi. 320, 2 advts. Cloth.

Contents

The Figure in the Carpet.
Originally appeared in *Cosmopolis*, January–February, 1896.
Glasses.
Originally appeared in the *Atlantic Monthly*, February, 1896.
The Next Time.
Originally appeared in the *Yellow Book*, July, 1895.
The Way It Came.
Originally appeared, simultaneously, in the *Chap Book*,
May 1, and in *Chapman's Magazine of Fiction*, May, 1896.

THE SAME. *First English Edition.*

EMBARRASSMENTS [in red] / THE
FIGURE IN THE / CARPET . . GLASS-
ES. / THE NEXT TIME . . / THE WAY
IT CAME . . / By Henry James / [orna-
ment] / London: William Heinemann [in red]
/ MDCCCXCVI.

Crown 8vo, pp. viii. 263, 1 blank, followed by
publishers' advertisements, pp. 32. Cloth.

For the first reprinting of *The Way It Came* under the title

"The Friends of the Friends," *see* Volume XVII of the New York Edition of the *Novels and Tales of Henry James*. For later reprintings under the same title, *see* the Index.
For reprintings of *The Figure in the Carpet* and *Glasses* as separate books, *see* the Index.
For reprintings of these tales in other collective volumes, *see* the Index.

THE OTHER HOUSE / By / Henry James / Author of "Daisy Miller," "The Europeans" / Etc., Etc. / New York / The Macmillan Company / London: Macmillan & Co., Ltd. / 1896 / All rights reserved.

12mo, pp. iv. 388, 3 advts., 1 blank. Cloth.

THE SAME. *First English Edition.*

THE OTHER HOUSE / By / Henry James / In Two Volumes / Vol. I. [II] / London / William Heinemann / 1896.

Globe 8vo. Vol. I. pp. iv. 206, 2 blanks, followed by publishers' advertisements, pp. 32. Vol. II. pp. iv. 202, 2 blanks, followed by publishers' advertisements, pp. 32. Cloth.

THE SAME. 1897.

London: William Heinemann.

For *The Other House*, as a tragedy in three acts, *see under* Unpublished Dramatic Works.

1897

THE SPOILS OF POYNTON / By / Henry James / [publishers' device] / Boston and New York / Houghton, Mifflin and Com-

pany / The Riverside Press, Cambridge / 1897.
[1896]

12mo, pp. iv. 323, 1 blank. Blank leaves at beginning and end. Cloth.

Originally appeared, under the title "The Old
Things," in the *Atlantic Monthly*, April–October, 1896.

THE SAME. *First English Edition.*

THE / SPOILS OF POYNTON [in red] /
By Henry James / Author of / "Terminations,"
"Embarrassments" / [ornament] / London:
William Heinemann [in red] / MDCCCXCVII.

Crown 8vo, pp. iv. 286, 1 advt., 1 blank, followed by publishers' advertisements, pp. 32.
Cloth.

For reprintings of *The Spoils of Poynton* in collective volumes, *see* the Index.

WHAT MAISIE KNEW / By / Henry
James / [publishers' device in red] / Herbert S.
Stone & Co. / Chicago & New York / MDCCC-
XCVII. [Entire title within a double line border]

12mo, pp. viii. 471, 5 blanks. Cloth.

Originally appeared, simultaneously, in the *Chap
Book*, January 15–August 1, and in the *New Review*,
February–July, 1897.

THE SAME. *First English Edition.*

WHAT MAISIE KNEW [in red] / By
Henry James / [ornament] / London: William
Heinemann [in red] / M DCCC XCVIII.

Crown 8vo, pp. iv. 304, followed by publishers' advertisements, pp. 32. Cloth.

For reprintings of *What Maisie Knew* in collective volumes, *see* the Index.

1898

THE TWO MAGICS / THE TURN OF THE SCREW / COVERING END / By / Henry James / Author of "Daisy Miller," "The Europeans" / Etc., Etc. / New York / The Macmillan Company / London: Macmillan & Co., Ltd. / 1898 / All rights reserved.

12mo, pp. iv. 393, 1 blank, 2 advts. Cloth.

Contents

The Turn of the Screw.
Originally appeared in *Collier's Weekly*, February 5–April 16, 1898.

Covering End.
This story appears here for the first time.
For unpublished dramatic versions of Covering End, *see under* Unpublished Dramatic Works.

THE SAME. *First English Edition.*

THE TWO MAGICS [in red] / THE TURN OF THE SCREW / COVERING END / By Henry James / [ornament] / London: William Heinemann [in red] / MDCCC-XCVIII.

Crown 8vo, pp. iv. 310, 2 blanks, followed by publishers' advertisements, pp. 32. Cloth.

For reprintings of *The Turn of the Screw* as a separate book, *see* the Index.

For reprintings of *The Turn of the Screw* in other collective volumes, *see* the Index.

IN THE CAGE / By / Henry James / [publishers' device in red] / Herbert S. Stone & Company / Chicago & New York / MDCCCXCVIII. [Entire title within a double line border]

12mo, pp. viii. 229, 1 blank, 1 printers' mark, 5 blanks. Cloth.

THE SAME. *First English Edition.*

IN THE CAGE / By / Henry James / [publishers' device] / London / Duckworth and Co. / 3 Henrietta Street, W.C. / 1898.

Crown 8vo, pp. iv. 187, 1 blank, 16 advts. Cloth.

THE SAME. 1819.

See under Uniform Edition of the Tales of Henry James.

For reprintings of *In the Cage* in collective volumes, *see* the Index.
A translation into French, in book form, of this story ("Dans la Cage") has been announced for early publication by Librairie Stock (Delamain et Boutelleau), Paris.

1899

[Two lines] / THE AWKWARD AGE / [two lines] / A Novel. By Henry James / Author of "Washington Square" / "Daisy Miller" "Picture and Text" / "Terminations" "The Private Life" / [two lines] / [publishers' device] /

[two lines] / Harper & Brothers Publishers / New York and London / 1899 / [two lines]
12mo, pp. iv. 457, 1 blank, 2 advts. Cloth.

Originally appeared in *Harper's Weekly*, October 1, 1898—January 7, 1899.

THE SAME. *First English Edition.*

THE AWKWARD AGE [in red] / By Henry James / Author of / "The Two Magics," "What Maisie Knew," / "The Spoils of Poynton," Etc., Etc. / [ornament] / London: William Heinemann [in red] / MDCCCXCIX.
Crown 8vo, pp. [ii], vi. 414, 2 advts., followed by publishers' advertisements, pp. 32. Cloth.

THE SAME. 1908.

See under Novels and Tales of Henry James, New York Edition.

THE SAME. 1922.

See under Novels and Stories of Henry James, New and Complete Edition.

1900

THE SOFT SIDE / By / Henry James / Author of "The Other House," "The / Two Magics," Etc. / New York / The Macmillan Company / London: Macmillan & Co., Ltd. / 1900 / All rights reserved.
12mo, pp. vi. 326, 3 advts., 1 blank. Cloth.

Contents

The Great Good Place.
  Originally appeared in *Scribner's Magazine*, January, 1900.

'Europe.'
  Originally appeared in *Scribner's Magazine*, June, 1899.

Paste.
  This tale appears here for the first time.

The Real Right Thing.
  This tale appears here for the first time.

The Great Condition.
  Originally appeared in the *Anglo-Saxon Review*, June, 1899.

The Tree of Knowledge.
  This tale appears here for the first time.

The Abasement of the Northmores.
  This tale appears here for the first time.

The Given Case.
  This tale appears here for the first time.

John Delavoy.
  Originally appeared in *Cosmopolis*, January–February, 1898.

The Third Person.
  This tale appears here for the first time.

Maud-Evelyn.
  Originally appeared in the *Atlantic Monthly*, April, 1900.

Miss Gunton of Poughkeepsie.
  Originally appeared in the *Cornhill Magazine*, May, 1900.

THE SAME. *First English Edition.*

THE SOFT SIDE / By / Henry James /
Methuen & Co. / 36 Essex Street W.C. / Lon-
don / 1900.
  Crown 8vo, pp. viii. 392. Cloth.

  For reprintings of these tales in other collective volumes, *see*
  the Index.

For a translation of *Paste* into French ("Perle Fausse") as a
contribution to a periodical, *see* the Index.

1901

THE SACRED FOUNT / By / Henry
James / New York / Charles Scribner's Sons /
1901.

12mo, pp. iv. 319, 1 blank. Cloth.

THE SAME. *First English Edition*.

THE SACRED FOUNT / By / Henry
James / Methuen & Co. / 36 Essex Street
W.C. / London / 1901.

Crown 8vo, pp. iv. 316, followed by publishers' advertisements, pp. 48. Cloth.

THE SAME. 1923.

See under Novels and Stories of Henry James, New
and Complete Edition.

1902

THE WINGS OF / THE DOVE / By /
Henry James / Volume I [II] / New York /
Charles Scribner's Sons / 1902.

12mo, Vol. I. pp. vi. 329, 3 blanks. Vol. II.
pp. vi. 439, 5 blanks. Cloth.

THE SAME. *First English Edition*.

THE / WINGS OF THE DOVE / By /
Henry James / [ornament] / Westminster /

Archibald Constable and Co., Ltd. / 2 White-
hall Gardens, S.W. / 1902.

Crown 8vo, pp. iv. 576, followed by publishers' advertisements, pp. 16. Cloth.

THE SAME. 1909.

See under Novels and Tales of Henry James, New
York Edition.

THE SAME. 1923.

See under Novels and Stories of Henry James, New
and Complete Edition.

1903

WILLIAM WETMORE STORY / AND
/ HIS FRIENDS / FROM LETTERS,
DIARIES, AND RECOLLECTIONS /
By / Henry James / In Two Volumes / Vol. I.
[II] / William Blackwood and Sons / Edin-
burgh and London / MCMIII / All Rights re-
served.

Post 8vo. Vol. I. pp. viii. 371, 1 blank. Portrait. Vol. II. pp. viii. 345, 3 blanks. Portrait.
Cloth.

Sheets of the English Edition were used for the Ameri-
can Edition. With the exception of the imprint of the
American publishers—Houghton, Mifflin & Company,
Boston—the two editions are identical.

THE BETTER SORT / By / Henry James
/ New York / Charles Scribner's Sons / 1903.

12mo, pp. viii. 429, 3 blanks. Cloth.

Contents

Broken Wings.
>Originally appeared in the *Century Magazine*, December, 1900.

The Beldonald Holbein.
>Originally appeared in *Harper's Magazine*, October, 1901.

The Two Faces.
>Originally appeared, under the title "The Faces," in *Harper's Bazar*, December 15, 1900.

The Tone of Time.
>Originally appeared in *Scribner's Magazine*, November, 1900.

The Special Type.
>This tale appears here for the first time.

Mrs. Medwin.
>Originally appeared in *Punch*, August 28–September 18, 1901.

Flickerbridge.
>Originally appeared in *Scribner's Magazine*, February, 1902.

The Story in It.
>In the Preface to Volume XVIII of his *Novels and Tales*, New York Edition, in which this tale is included, Henry James indicates that *The Story in It* first appeared in 1903, in the first number of a magazine which was, "if I mistake not, to prove only one of a pair." The name of the periodical and the exact date of its appearance are not established.

The Beast in the Jungle.
>This tale appears here for the first time.

The Birthplace.
>This tale appears here for the first time.

The Papers.
>This tale appears here for the first time.

THE SAME. *First English Edition.*

THE BETTER SORT / By / Henry James / Methuen & Co. / 36 Essex Street W.C. / London / 1903.

Crown 8vo, pp. vi. 312, followed by publishers' advertisements, pp. 40. Cloth.

For a reprinting of *The Beast in the Jungle* as a separate book, *see* the Index.
For reprintings of these tales in other collective volumes, *see* the Index.

THE AMBASSADORS [in red] / A Novel / by / Henry James / Author of "The Awkward Age" "Daisy Miller" / "An International Episode" Etc. / [publishers' device] / New York and London / Harper & Brothers Publishers / MCMIII.

8vo, pp. ii. 432. Boards, with cloth jacket.

Originally appeared in the *North American Review*, January–December, 1903.

THE SAME. *First English Edition.*

THE AMBASSADORS / By / Henry James / Methuen & Co. / 36 Essex Street W.C. / London / 1903.

Crown 8vo, pp. iv. 459, 1 blank, followed by publishers' advertisements, pp. 40. Cloth.

THE SAME. 1909.

See under Novels and Tales of Henry James, New York Edition.

THE SAME. 1923.

See under Novels and Stories of Henry James, New and Complete Edition.

1904

THE GOLDEN BOWL / By / Henry James / Volume I [II] / New York / Charles Scribner's Sons / 1904.

12mo. Vol. I. pp. iv. 412. Vol. II. pp. iv. 377, 3 blanks. Cloth.

THE SAME. *First English Edition.*

THE GOLDEN BOWL / By / Henry James / Methuen & Co. / 36 Essex Street W.C. / London / [1905]

Crown 8vo, pp. viii. 548, followed by publishers' advertisements, pp. 40. Cloth.

THE SAME. 1909.

See under Novels and Tales of Henry James, New York Edition.

THE SAME. 1923.

See under Novels and Stories of Henry James, New and Complete Edition.

1905

THE QUESTION OF OUR / SPEECH / THE LESSON OF BALZAC / Two Lectures / By Henry James / [publishers' device in brown] / Boston and New York / Houghton, Mifflin and Company / The Riverside Press, Cambridge / 1905.

Narrow 12mo, pp. viii. 118. Cloth.

Contents

The Question of Our Speech.

Originally appeared in *Appleton's Booklovers' Magazine*, August, 1905.

The following note appears on page 3. "Address to the graduating class at Bryn Mawr College, Pennsylvania, June 8, 1905; here printed with the restoration of a few passages omitted on that occasion."

The Lesson of Balzac.

Originally appeared in the *Atlantic Monthly*, August, 1905. The following note appears on page 55. "Delivered for the first time before the Contemporary Club of Philadelphia, January 12, 1905, and repeated on various occasions elsewhere. Several passages omitted on delivery—one of considerable length—have been restored."

Of the first edition, three hundred copies were bound entirely uncut in boards, with cloth back and paper label.

ENGLISH HOURS [in red] / By Henry James / With Illustrations / By Joseph Pennell / [illustration] / Boston and New York / Houghton, Mifflin and Company / The Riverside Press, Cambridge [in red] / MDCCCCV.

Crown 8vo, pp. [iv], xiv (with an inserted leaf, unpaged, between pp. vi and [vii]). 338. Plates. Cloth.

Contents

London.

Browning in Westminster Abbey.

Chester.

Lichfield and Warwick.

North Devon.

Wells and Salisbury.

An English Easter.

London at Midsummer.

Two Excursions.

In Warwickshire.

Abbeys and Castles.

English Vignettes.

An English New Year.

An English Watering-Place.

Winchelsea, Rye and "Denis Duval."
> Originally appeared in *Scribner's Magazine*, January, 1901.

Old Suffolk.
> Originally appeared in *Harper's Weekly*, September 25, 1897. By a misprint, in both the American and English editions, the year of the original appearance of *Old Suffolk* is given as "1879."

> For the original appearance and first reprinting in a book, *see under* Essays in London and Elsewhere for the following papers;—London, Browning in Westminster Abbey.
> For the original appearance and first reprinting in a book, *see under* Transatlantic Sketches for the following papers; —Chester, Lichfield and Warwick, North Devon, Wells and Salisbury.
> For the original appearance and first reprinting in a book, *see under* Portraits of Places for the following papers;— An English Easter, London at Midsummer, Two Excursions, In Warwickshire, Abbeys and Castles, English Vignettes, An English New Year, An English Watering-Place.
> A large paper issue of *English Hours*, in the American Edition, was limited to four hundred copies.

THE SAME. *First English Edition.*

ENGLISH HOURS / By / Henry James / [illustration] / With Ninety-two Illustrations

by / Joseph Pennell / London / William Heinemann / 1905.
Post 4to, pp. xii. 315, 1 blank. Plates. Cloth.

1907

THE / AMERICAN SCENE / By / Henry
James / [publishers' device] / Harper & Brothers Publishers / New York and London /
MCMVII.
8vo, pp. [ii], viii. 443, 3 blanks. Cloth.

Contents

I. New England: An Autumn Impression.
Originally appeared in the *North American Review*, April–
June, 1905.

II. New York Revisited.
Originally appeared in *Harper's Magazine*, February–March,
and May, 1906.

III. New York and the Hudson: A Spring Impression.
Originally appeared in the *North American Review*, December, 1905.

IV. New York: Social Notes.
Originally appeared in the *North American Review*, January–February, 1906. Also in the *Fortnightly Review*, February, 1906.

V. The Bowery and Thereabouts.
No previous appearance of this paper has been recorded.

VI. The Sense of Newport.
Originally appeared in *Harper's Magazine*, August, 1906.

VII. Boston.
Originally appeared in the *North American Review* and the
Fortnightly Review, March, 1906.

VIII. Concord and Salem.
No previous appearance of this paper has been recorded.

IX. Philadelphia.
Originally appeared in the *North American Review* and the *Fortnightly Review*, April, 1906.

X. Baltimore.
Originally appeared in the *North American Review*, August, 1906.

XI. Washington.
Originally appeared in the *North American Review*, May–June, 1906.

XII. Richmond.
Originally appeared, under the title "Richmond, Virginia," in the *Fortnightly Review*, November, 1906.

XIII. Charleston.
No previous appearance of this paper has been recorded.

XIV. Florida.
No previous appearance of this paper has been recorded.

THE SAME. *First English Edition.*

THE AMERICAN SCENE / By / Henry James / London / Chapman and Hall, Ltd / 1907.
Demy 8vo, pp. viii. 466, 6 advts. Cloth.

The Contents pages of the American and English editions are the same. The Preface of the American Edition is dated September 28, 1906, while that of the English Edition is undated. The text of the American Edition ends on page 460 of the English Edition. Some of the text on page 460 of the English Edition, and all which follows, is not included in the American Edition.

1908

VIEWS / AND REVIEWS / By / Henry James / Now First Collected / Introduction By

/ LeRoy Phillips / Compiler of / "A Bibliography of the Writings / of Henry James" / Boston / The Ball Publishing Company / 1908. 12mo, pp. xiv. 241, 1 blank. Cloth.

Contents

The Novels of George Eliot.
Originally appeared in the *Atlantic Monthly*, October, 1866.

On a Drama of Robert Browning.
Originally appeared, under the title "Robert Browning's 'Inn Album,'" in the *Nation*, January 20, 1876.

Swinburne's Essays.
Originally appeared, under the title "Algernon Charles Swinburne's Essays and Studies," in the *Nation*, July 29, 1875.

The Poetry of William Morris.
Originally appeared, under the titles "William Morris' 'The Life and Death of Jason: A Poem,'" in the *North American Review*, October, 1867; and "William Morris' 'The Earthly Paradise: A Poem,'" in the *Nation*, July 9, 1868.

Matthew Arnold's Essays.
Originally appeared, under the title "Matthew Arnold's 'Essays in Criticism,'" in the *North American Review*, July, 1865.

Mr. Walt Whitman.
Originally appeared in the *Nation*, November 16, 1865.

The Poetry of George Eliot.
Originally appeared under the titles "George Eliot's 'Spanish Gypsy: A Poem,'" in the *North American Review*, October, 1868; and "George Eliot's 'The Legend of Jubal, and Other Poems,'" in the same periodical, October, 1874.

The Limitations of Dickens.
Originally appeared, under the title "Charles Dickens' 'Our Mutual Friend,'" in the *Nation*, December 21, 1865.

Tennyson's Drama.
Originally appeared, under the titles "Mr. Tennyson's Drama" (Review of "Queen Mary"), in the *Galaxy*, Sep-

tember, 1875; and "Mr. Tennyson's New Drama" (Review of "Harold: A Drama"), in the *Nation*, January 18, 1877.

Contemporary Notes on Whistler vs. Ruskin.
Originally appeared, under the title "Whistler," in the *Nation*, December 19, 1878; and, in the same periodical, February 13, 1879.

A Note on John Burroughs.
Originally appeared, under the title "John Burroughs' 'Winter Sunshine,'" in the *Nation*, January 27, 1876.

Mr. Kipling's Early Stories.
Originally appeared as a Critical Introduction to *Soldiers Three*, The English Library, Volume LIX, 1891.

Of the first edition, one hundred and sixty numbered copies were bound in vellum.

1909

JULIA BRIDE [in red] / By / Henry James / Illustrated by / W. T. Smedley / [publishers' device] / New York and London / Harper & Brothers Publishers [in red] / MCMIX. [Entire title within a triple line border; the inner line black, the two outer lines, close together, red]

8vo, pp. viii. 84, 4 blanks. Frontispiece and three full-page illustrations inserted.

Originally appeared in *Harper's Magazine*, March–April, 1908.

For reprintings of *Julia Bride* in collective volumes, *see* the Index.

ITALIAN HOURS / By Henry James / With Illustrations in Color / By Joseph Pennell / [publishers' device in red] / Boston and New York / Houghton Mifflin Company / MDCCCCIX.

Demi 4to, pp. x. 506. Colored plates. Cloth.
Boxed.

Contents

Venice.

The Grand Canal.

Venice: An Early Impression.

Two Old Houses and Three Young Women.

Casa Alvisi.

From Chambéry to Milan.

The Old Saint-Gothard.

Italy Revisited.

A Roman Holiday.

Roman Rides.

Roman Neighbourhoods.

The After-Season in Rome.

From a Roman Note-Book.

A Few Other Roman Neighbourhoods.

A Chain of Cities.

Siena Early and Late.

The Autumn in Florence.

Florentine Notes.

Tuscan Cities.

Other Tuscan Cities.

Ravenna.

The Saint's Afternoon and Others.

THE SAME. *First English Edition.*

ITALIAN HOURS [in brown] / By / Henry James / Author of "English Hours," "A Little Tour in France," Etc. / Illustrated by Joseph Pennell / [publishers' device] / London / William Heinemann / 1909. Crown 4to, pp. xii. 376. Colored plates. Buckram.

In his Preface, Henry James indicates that, with few exceptions, these impressions have already been collected in other volumes. The earlier text has been amended and a few passages have been included which refer to later visits to Italy. The dates of composition are shown at the ends of most of the chapters.

For the original appearance and first reprinting in a book of the following chapters, *see under* Transatlantic Sketches. Venice: An Early Impression, under the title, "From Venice to Strasburg." From Chambéry to Milan. The Old Saint-Gothard, under the title, "The St. Gothard." A Roman Holiday. Roman Rides. Roman Neighbourhoods. The After-Season in Rome. From a Roman Note-Book. A Chain of Cities, under the title, "A Chain of Italian Cities." The first part of Siena Early and Late, under the title, "Siena." The Autumn in Florence. Florentine Notes. Tuscan Cities. Ravenna.

For the original appearance and first reprinting in a book of *Venice* and *Italy Revisited*, *see under* Portraits of Places.

For the original appearance and first reprinting in a book of *The Grand Canal*, *see under* The Great Streets of the World.

For the original appearance of the first part of *The Saint's Afternoon and Others*, *see under* The May Book.

Castle Alvisi originally appeared in the *Cornhill Magazine* and *The Critic*, February, 1902, as a "Prefatory Note" to *Browning in Venice*. It is here reprinted in a book for the first time.

The following chapters, or parts of chapters, first appear in *Italian Hours;*—Two Old Houses and Three Young Women. A Few Other Roman Neighbourhoods. The last part of Siena Early and Late. Other Tuscan Cities. The last part of The Saint's Afternoon and Others.

1910

THE FINER GRAIN / By / Henry James / New York / Charles Scribner's Sons / 1910. 12mo, pp. viii. 312. Cloth.

Contents

The Velvet Glove.
> Originally appeared in the *English Review*, March, 1909.

Mora Montravers.
> Originally appeared in the *English Review*, August–September, 1909.

A Round of Visits.
> Originally appeared in the *English Review*, April–May, 1910.

Crapy Cornelia.
> Originally appeared in *Harper's Magazine*, October, 1909.

The Bench of Desolation.
> Originally appeared in *Putnam's Magazine*, October, 1909— January, 1910.

THE SAME. *First English Edition.*

THE / FINER GRAIN / By / Henry James / Methuen & Co. Ltd. / 36 Essex Street W.C. / London / [1910]

Crown 8vo, pp. viii. 308, followed by publishers' advertisements, pp. 32. Cloth.

THE SAME. 1910.

Published in *Collection of British Authors*, Volume 4224. Leipzig: Bernhard Tauchnitz.

For a reprinting of these tales in a collective volume, *see* the Index.

1911

THE / HENRY JAMES / YEAR BOOK / Selected and Arranged by / Evelyn Garnaut Smalley / With an Introduction by / Henry James and William Dean Howells / [publishers' device] / Richard G. Badger / The Gorham Press / Boston / [1911] [Entire title in black, within four single line panels in red]

12mo, 122 leaves, no page numerals. Portrait. Cloth.

The text is in black, within paneled borders in red.

Henry James's "Introduction I. The Author to the Public," dated London, June 16, 1910, is on page [9].

Sheets of the American Edition were used for the English Edition, which has the imprint of J. M. Dent & Sons, London.

THE OUTCRY / By / Henry James / New York / Charles Scribner's Sons / 1911.

12mo, pp. vi. 261, 1 blank. Cloth.

THE SAME. *First English Edition.*

THE OUTCRY / By / Henry James / Methuen & Co. Ltd. / 36 Essex Street W.C. / London / [1911]

Crown 8vo, pp. vi. 312, followed by publishers' advertisements, pp. 32.

THE SAME. 1912.

Published in *Collection of British Authors*, Volume 4308. Leipzig: Bernhard Tauchnitz.

The *Outcry* was originally written as a comedy in three acts. As such it was unpublished and no printed copies of the stage version, from which it was converted into fiction, have been recorded. *See under* Unpublished Dramatic Works.

1913

A SMALL BOY / AND OTHERS / By / Henry James / New York / Charles Scribner's Sons / 1913.

8vo, pp. vi. 419, 1 blank. Frontispiece. Cloth.

THE SAME. *First English Edition.*

A SMALL BOY / AND OTHERS / By / Henry James / Macmillan and Co., Limited / St. Martin's Street, London / 1913.

8vo, pp. iv. 436, 1 blank, 3 advts., 2 blanks. Frontispiece. Cloth.

1914

NOTES ON NOVELISTS / With Some Other Notes / By / Henry James / New York / Charles Scribner's Sons / 1914.

8vo, pp. viii. 455, 1 blank. Cloth.

Contents

An American Art-Scholar: Charles Eliot Norton, 1908.
No previous appearance of this paper has been recorded.

London Notes, January, 1897.
Originally appeared, under the title "London," in *Harper's Weekly*, February 6, 1897.

London Notes, June, 1897.
Originally appeared, under the title "London," in *Harper's Weekly*, June 26, 1897.

London Notes, July, 1897.
Originally appeared, under the title "London," in *Harper's Weekly*, July 31, 1897.

London Notes, August, 1897.
Originally appeared, under the title "London," in *Harper's Weekly*, August 21, 1897.

THE SAME. *First English Edition.*

NOTES ON NOVELISTS [in red] / With / Some Other Notes / By / Henry James / [publishers' device] / MCMXIV / J. M. Dent & Sons Ltd. [in red] / Aldine House, Bedford St., W.C.
Small demi 8vo, pp. viii. 360. Cloth.

NOTES OF A / SON AND BROTHER / By / Henry James / Illustrated / New York / Charles Scribner's Sons / 1914.
8vo, pp. x. 515, 3 blanks. Frontispiece. Plates. Cloth.

THE SAME. *First English Edition.*

NOTES / OF / A SON & BROTHER / By / Henry James / Macmillan and Co., Limited / St. Martin's Street, London / 1914.

8vo, pp. viii. 479, 1 blank, 2 advts. Frontispiece. Plates. Cloth.

THE AMERICAN VOLUNTEER / MO-
TOR-AMBULANCE CORPS / In France /
A Letter to the Editor of An American Journal
/ By / Henry James / Macmillan and Co.,
Limited / St. Martin's Street, London / 1914 /
Price One Penny.

8vo, pp. 12. First cover-page serves as title-
page. Wrappers.

1915

England / at War: / An Essay / THE QUES-
TION OF THE MIND / By / Henry James
/ Issued by / The Central Committee / For Na-
tional Patriotic Organization / C. P. Building,
62 Charing Cross, London. W.C. / Price One
Penny. / [1915]

8½ x 5½ inches, pp. 20. First cover-page
serves as title-page. No wrappers.

"The Question of the Mind" is on pages 3–12, with
the name of Henry James at the close. "England," by
A. Clutton-Brock (from the *Times Literary Supplement*,
November 19, 1914), is on pages 13–20.

1916

PICTURES / AND OTHER PASSAGES
FROM / HENRY JAMES / [ornament] /
Selected By / Ruth Head / London / Chatto
and Windus / [1916]

Small crown 8vo, pp. xiv. 136. Boards, cloth back with paper label.

The Preface, dated May 28, 1916, includes a letter from Henry James addressed to the compiler.

Sheets of the English Edition were used for the American Edition, which has the imprint of Frederick A. Stokes Company, New York.

LETTERS / TO / AN EDITOR / By / Henry James.

9 x 7⅜ inches, pp. 16. Wrappers.

The following is on the reverse of the title-page,—"Of this little book, containing hitherto unpublished letters by Henry James, twenty-five copies only have been privately printed by Clement Shorter for distribution among his friends. London, April 1st, 1916."

The letters by Henry James, addressed to Clement Shorter, include pages 5–12.

1917

THE IVORY TOWER / By Henry James / New York / Charles Scribner's Sons / 1917.

12mo, pp. [ii], viii. 357, 1 blank. Cloth.

THE SAME. *First English Edition.*

THE IVORY TOWER / By / Henry James / London: 48 Pall Mall / W. Collins Sons & Co. Ltd. / Glasgow Melbourne Auckland / [1917]

Extra crown 8vo, pp. viii. 348. Portrait. Cloth.

In a Preface, Percy Lubbock states that this is one of

the two novels which Henry James left unfinished at his death.

The plates of the first American Edition of *The Ivory Tower* were used in printing a supplementary volume for the New York Edition of *The Novels and Tales of Henry James.*

THE / SENSE OF THE PAST / By / Henry James / New York / Charles Scribner's Sons / 1917.

12mo, pp. x. 358. Cloth.

THE SAME. *First English Edition.*

THE SENSE OF / THE PAST / By / Henry James / London: 48 Pall Mall / W. Collins Sons & Co. Ltd. / Glasgow Melbourne Auckland / [1917]

Extra crown 8vo, pp. viii. 351, 1 blank. Portrait. Cloth.

In a Preface, Percy Lubbock states that this is one of the two novels which Henry James left unfinished at his death.

The plates of the first American Edition of *The Sense of the Past* were used in printing a supplementary volume for the New York Edition of *The Novels and Tales of Henry James.*

THE / MIDDLE YEARS / By / Henry James / New York / Charles Scribner's Sons / 1917.

8vo, pp. [viii] 119, 1 blank. Portrait. Cloth.

THE SAME. *First English Edition.*

THE / MIDDLE YEARS / By / Henry
James / London: 48 Pall Mall / W. Collins
Sons & Co. Ltd. / Glasgow Melbourne Auck-
land / [1917]
  Extra crown 8vo, pp. [viii] 118, 2 blanks.
Portrait. Cloth.

  Percy Lubbock, in an Editor's Note, states that this
was the beginning of a volume of autobiographical reminiscences which Henry James left unfinished at his death.
The title (*see* the Index) is one which the author used
for one of his own short stories.
  This fragment of a projected book also appeared in
Scribner's Magazine, October–November, 1917.

1918

WITHIN THE RIM / and Other Essays /
1914–15 / Henry James / [publishers' device] /
London: 48 Pall Mall / W. Collins Sons & Co.
Ltd. / Glasgow Melbourne Auckland / [1918]
  Extra crown 8vo, pp. 119, 1 blank. Cloth.

Contents

Within the Rim.
  Originally appeared in the *Fortnightly Review*, August,
  1917. Within the Rim was written in February, 1915, as a
  contribution to a proposed album in aid of the Arts Fund.
  The idea of the album was abandoned.

Refugees in Chelsea.
  Originally appeared in the *Times Literary Supplement*,
  March 23, 1916.

The American Volunteer Motor-Ambulance Corps in
France: A Letter to the Editor of an American Journal.
  Originally appeared, 1914, as a separate pamphlet.

France.
> For original appearance and first reprinting in a book, *see under* The Book of France.

The Long Wards.
> For original appearance and first reprinting in a book, *see under* The Book of the Homeless.

> For a reprinting of *Refugees in Chelsea* as a separate book, *see* the Index.

GABRIELLE DE BERGERAC / By Henry James / [publishers' device] / New York / Boni and Liveright / 1918.

12mo, pp. 153, 3 blanks. Boards, cloth back.

Originally appeared in the *Atlantic Monthly*, July–September, 1869.

1919

A LANDSCAPE / PAINTER / By / Henry James / [publishers' device] / New York / Scott and Seltzer / 1919.

12mo, pp. vi. 287, 3 blanks. Cloth.

Contents

A Landscape Painter.
> For original appearance and first reprinting in a book, *see under* Stories Revived. Volume II.

Poor Richard.
> For original appearance and first reprinting in a book, *see under* Stories Revived. Volume III.

A Day of Days.
> For original appearance and first reprinting in a book, *see under* Stories Revived. Volume I.

A Most Extraordinary Case.
> For original appearance and first reprinting in a book, *see*
> *under* Stories Revived. Volume III.

> Pages 1–4 include a Preface by Albert Mordell in which he
> states that the tales comprising this volume are printed now
> for the first time in America in book form.
> A special issue of the first edition of *A Landscape Painter*
> was limited to two hundred and fifty copies.
> For reprintings of these tales in other collective volumes, *see*
> the Index.

TRAVELLING / COMPANIONS / By / Henry James / [publishers' device] / Boni and Liveright / New York 1919.

12mo, pp. x. 309, 1 blank. Cloth.

Contents

Travelling Companions.
> Originally appeared in the *Atlantic Monthly*, November–
> December, 1870.

The Sweetheart of M. Briseux.
> Originally appeared in the *Galaxy*, June, 1873.

Professor Fargo.
> Originally appeared in the *Galaxy*, August, 1874.

At Isella.
> Originally appeared in the *Galaxy*, August, 1871.

Guest's Confession.
> Originally appeared in the *Atlantic Monthly*, October–No-
> vember, 1872.

Adina.
> Originally appeared in *Scribner's Monthly*, May–June, 1874.

DeGrey: A Romance.
> Originally appeared in the *Atlantic Monthly*, July, 1868.

> Pages vii–ix include a Foreword by Albert Mordell in which
> he states that the stories in this volume are printed now for
> the first time in book form in America.

1920

MASTER EUSTACE / By / Henry James / [publishers' device] / New York / Thomas Seltzer / 1920.

12mo, pp. vi. 280, 2 blanks. Cloth.

Contents

Master Eustace.

> For original appearance and first reprinting in a book, *see under* Stories Revived. Volume III.

Longstaff's Marriage.

> For original appearance and first reprinting in a book, *see under* The Madonna of the Future and Other Tales. Volume I.

Théodolinde.

> For original appearance and first reprinting in a book, *see* "Rose-Agathe," *under* Stories Revived. Volume II.

A Light Man.

> For original appearance and first reprinting in a book, *see under* Stories by American Authors. V.

Benvolio.

> For original appearance and first reprinting in a book, *see under* The Madonna of the Future and Other Tales. Volume II.

> Pages 1–4 include a Preface by Albert Mordell in which he indicates that the tales comprising this volume are printed now for the first time in America in book form. Volume V, of *Stories by American Authors*, New York, 1894, included A Light Man.

THE LETTERS / OF / HENRY JAMES / Selected and Edited by / Percy Lubbock / Volume I [II] / New York / Charles Scribner's Sons / 1920.

8vo. Vol. I. pp. xxxiv. 434. Portrait. Vol. II.
pp. xiv. 511, 3 blanks. Portrait. Plate. Cloth.

The publishers bound a few copies of the first American Edition of *The Letters of Henry James* to match *The Novels and Tales of Henry James*, the New York Edition.

THE SAME. *First English Edition.*

THE LETTERS / OF / HENRY JAMES / Selected and Edited by / Percy Lubbock / Volume I [II] / Macmillan and Co., Limited / St. Martin's Street, London / 1920.

8vo. Vol. I. pp. xxxii. 442, 2 blanks. Portrait. Vol. II. pp. xii. 529, 3 blanks. Portrait. Plate. Cloth.

REFUGEES IN CHELSEA. Chelsea: The Ashendene Press.

Privately printed, six copies on vellum and fifty on paper.

For original appearance and first reprinting in a book, *see under* Within the Rim and Other Essays.

1921

NOTES AND REVIEWS / By / Henry James [in red] / With a Preface by Pierre de Chaignon la Rose / [line] / A Series of Twenty-five Papers Hith- / erto Unpublished in Book Form / [line] / [publishers' device] / [line] / Dunster House [in red] / Cambridge, Massachusetts / MDCCCCXXI.

8¾ x 6 inches, pp. xx. 227, 1 blank. Boards, cloth back.

Contents

I. Fiction and Sir Walter Scott.
   Originally appeared in the *North American Review*, October, 1864.

II. Miss Prescott's "Azarian."
   Originally appeared in the *North American Review*, January, 1865.

III. Lindisfarn Chase.
   Originally appeared in the *North American Review*, January, 1865.

IV. Emily Chester: A Novel.
   Originally appeared in the *North American Review*, January, 1865.

V. Miss Alcott's "Moods."
   Originally appeared in the *North American Review*, July, 1865.

VI. The Noble School of Fiction.
   Originally appeared in the *Nation*, July 6, 1865.

VII. "Miss Mac Kenzie."
   Originally appeared in the *Nation*, July 13, 1865.

VIII. "The Schönberg-Cotta Family."
   Originally appeared in the *Nation*, September 14, 1865.

IX. "Can You Forgive Her?"
   Originally appeared in the *Nation*, September 28, 1865.

X. "The Gayworthys."
   Originally appeared in the *North American Review*, October, 1865.

XI. A French Critic.
   Originally appeared in the *Nation*, October 12, 1865.

XII. Miss Braddon.
   Originally appeared in the *Nation*, November 9, 1865.

XIII. Eugénie de Guérin's Journal.
   Originally appeared in the *Nation*, December 14, 1865.

XIV. "The Belton Estate."
Originally appeared in the *Nation*, January 4, 1866.

XV. Swinburne's "Chastelard."
Originally appeared in the *Nation*, January 18, 1866.

XVI. Kingsley's "Hereward."
Originally appeared in the *Nation*, January 25, 1866.

XVII. "Winifred Bertram."
Originally appeared in the *Nation*, February 1, 1866.

XVIII. Mrs. Gaskell.
Originally appeared in the *Nation*, February 22, 1866.

XIX. "Marian Rooke."
Originally appeared in the *Nation*, February 22, 1866.

XX. "A Noble Life."
Originally appeared in the *Nation*, March 1, 1866.

XXI. Epictetus.
Originally appeared in the *North American Review*, April, 1866.

XXII. Victor Hugo's Last Novel.
Originally appeared in the *Nation*, April 12, 1866.

XXIII. Felix Holt, The Radical.
Originally appeared in the *Nation*, August 16, 1866.

XXIV. Eugéne de Guérin's Letters.
Originally appeared in the *Nation*, September 13, 1866.

XXV. The Last French Novel.
Originally appeared in the *Nation*, October 11, 1886.

A LETTER / FROM / HENRY JAMES / TO / MRS. LINTON / Privately Printed.

4¾ x 6¼ inches. Eight leaves of text paper. Wrappers.

A note, ending on the fifth leaf, is initialed, "G.P.W.," and dated, "December 1921," both in ink.

The letter from Henry James is on leaves 6 and 7.

The following is on the last leaf,—"This letter has been put into type on the fifty-first anniversary of the inception of a great novelist's happiest romance, at The Sign of The George."

1923

"A MOST UNHOLY TRADE" / Being Letters on the / Drama by Henry James / [ornament] / The Scarab Press / Privately Printed / MCMXXIII.

6' x 4½ inches. Between end papers, which are of text paper, are 14 leaves. Portrait. Paper boards, cloth back.

The first leaf is blank. The numbering of pages begins with the second leaf. The letters by Henry James include pages 7–18. Page 19, the last type page, is followed by 7 blank pages.

One hundred copies for sale at Dunster House, Cambridge, Massachusetts.

1926

[Entire title within single line panel] THREE LETTERS / from / HENRY JAMES / to JOSEPH CONRAD.

5½ x 8½ inches. 6 leaves of text paper. First cover-page serves as title-page. No wrappers. Inclosed in portfolio with letters from other authors addressed to Joseph Conrad.

The following is on the reverse of the first cover-page, —"220 copies of these letters from Henry James to Joseph Conrad have been printed for the First Edition Club, London, 1926, at the Crown Press."

THE TURN OF THE SCREW. London: Martin Secker.

Published in New Adelphi Library.

For previous printings of *The Turn of the Screw* in separate and in collective volumes, *see* the Index.

THE ASPERN PAPERS. London: Martin Secker.

Published in New Adelphi Library.

For previous printings in separate and in collective volumes and a translation into French of *The Aspern Papers, see* the Index.

1928

LETTERS OF HENRY JAMES TO WALTER BERRY [Italics, upper and lower case, in red] / The Black Sun Press / Editions Narcisse [in red] / Rue Cardinale / Paris [in red] / MCMXXVIII.

10¾ x 9⅛ inches. Between end papers, which are of text paper, are 32 leaves and an inserted supplementary letter (original or facsimile). Wrappers, with transparent jacket. Portfolio case.

The following is on the last printed leaf,—"This first edition of The Letters of Henry James to Walter Berry printed at the Black Sun Press (Maître Imprimeur Lescaret) Paris October 1928 for Harry and Caresse Crosby is strictly limited to 16 copies on Japan Paper and each copy supplemented by one of the original letters, and 100 numbered copies on Hollande Van Gelder Zonen to be sold at the Bookshop of Harry Marks, New York."

Since 1928 the reprintings of tales by Henry James include: in 1929, The Great Condition, *Golden Book Magazine*, December; in 1930, The Turn of the Screw and The Lesson of the Master, New York: The Modern Library, Number 169. Translations into French of tales by Henry James include: in 1929, Le Tour d'Écrou suivi de Les Papiers de Jeffroy Aspern (Translations of *The Turn of the Screw* and *The Aspern Papers*), Paris: Librairie Stock (Delamain et Boutelleau) and La Bête dans la Jungle (Translation of The Beast in the Jungle), Paris: Victor Attinger.

PART II

Contributions to Books

CONTRIBUTIONS TO BOOKS

1884

STORIES BY / AMERICAN AUTHORS / V. / [The titles of the stories and the names of the authors are within a single line border] A LIGHT MAN. / By Henry James. / YATIL. / By F. D. Millet. / THE END OF NEW YORK. / By Park Benjamin. / WHY THOMAS WAS DISCHARGED. / By George Arnold. / THE TACHYPOMP. / By E. P. Mitchell. / New York / Charles Scribner's Sons / 1884.

16mo, pp. 191, 1 blank, followed by publishers' advertisements, pp. 8. Cloth.

Henry James's contribution, "A Light Man," pp. 5–53, originally appeared in the *Galaxy*, July, 1869.

1885

Walter Besant / [line] / THE / ART OF FICTION / Boston / Cupples, Upham and Company / 1885.

12mo, pp. 85, 1 blank, followed by publishers' advertisements, pp. 5, 1 blank. Cloth.

The name of Henry James does not appear on the title-page of the first edition of *The Art of Fiction* in which his contribution, pp. 51–85, is included. On the cover his name appears with that of Walter Besant. This paper by Henry James originally appeared in *Longman's*

Magazine, September, 1884. It is a reply to Walter Besant's lecture, previously published as a book and similarly entitled, which was delivered at the Royal Institution, April 25, 1884.

1890

THE / ART OF AUTHORSHIP / LITERARY REMINISCENCES, / METHODS OF WORK, AND ADVICE TO YOUNG BEGINNERS, / Personally Contributed By / Leading Authors of the Day. / Compiled and Edited by / George Bainton. / London: / James Clarke & Co., 13 & 14, Fleet Street. / [line] / 1890.

Crown 8vo, pp. xii. 356, followed by publishers' advertisements, pp. 8. Cloth.

Henry James's contribution is on page 208. Plates of this edition were used in printing the American Edition which has the imprint of D. Appleton and Company, New York. The first American Edition is dated 1891.

1892

THE GREAT STREETS / OF / THE WORLD / By / Richard Harding Davis W. W. Story / Andrew Lang Henry James / Francisque Sarcey Paul Lindau / Isabel F. Hapgood / Illustrated by / A. B. Frost Ettore Tito / W. Douglas Almond Alexander Zezzos / G. Jeanniot F. Stahl / Ilya Efimovitch Répin / New York / Charles Scribner's Sons / 1892.

Large 8vo, pp. [ii], xiv. 253, 3 blanks, with blank leaves at beginning and end. Cloth.

Henry James's contribution, "The Grand Canal," pp. 143–172, originally appeared in *Scribner's Magazine*, November, 1892.

Sheets of this edition were used for the English Edition, which has the imprint of James R. Osgood, McIlvaine & Co., London.

1897

LIBRARY / OF THE / WORLD'S BEST LITERATURE / Ancient and Modern / Charles Dudley Warner / Editor / Hamilton Wright Mabie, Lucia Gilbert Runkle, / George H. Warner / Associate Editors / Thirty Volumes / Vol. XII / New York / R. S. Peale and J. A. Hill / Publishers. / [1897]

8vo, pp. [iv], xiv. 6653–7246, 4 blanks. Portraits. Various bindings.

Henry James's contribution, "Nathaniel Hawthorne," includes pp. 7053–7061.

LIBRARY OF THE WORLD'S BEST LITERATURE Ancient and Modern. Charles Dudley Warner Editor. Hamilton Wright Mabie, Lucia Gilbert Runkle, George H. Warner, Associate Editors. Volume XIV.

New York: R. S. Peale and J. A. Hill.

Henry James's contribution, "The Madonna of the Future," includes pp. 8075–8109. For original appearance and first reprinting in a book, *see under* A Passionate Pilgrim and Other Tales.

LIBRARY / OF THE / WORLD'S BEST LITERATURE / Ancient and Modern / Charles Dudley Warner / Editor / Hamilton Wright Mabie, Lucia Gilbert Runkle, / George H. Warner / Associate Editors / Thirty Volumes / Vol. XVI / New York / R. S. Peale and J. A. Hill / Publishers. / [1897]
    8vo, pp. [iv], xiv. 9025–9616, 6 blanks. Portraits. Various bindings.
    Henry James's contribution, "James Russell Lowell," includes pp. 9229–9237.

LIBRARY / OF THE / WORLD'S BEST LITERATURE / Ancient and Modern / Charles Dudley Warner / Editor / Hamilton Wright Mabie, Lucia Gilbert Runkle, / George H. Warner / Associate Editors / Thirty Volumes / Vol. XXV / New York / R. S. Peale and J. A. Hill / Publishers. / [1897]
    8vo, pp. [iv], xiv. 14469–15090, 4 blanks. Portraits. Various bindings.
    Henry James's contribution, "Ivan Turgeneff," includes pp. 15057–15062.

1898

THE INTERNATIONAL LIBRARY OF FAMOUS LITERATURE. Edited by

Donald G. Mitchell and Andrew Lang. Volume
XVIII.
New York: Merrill and Baker.

Henry James's contribution, "The Romance of Certain Old Clothes," includes pp. 8677–8696. For original
appearance and first reprinting in a book, *see under* A
Passionate Pilgrim and Other Tales.

1899

THE WARNER CLASSICS. THE NOV-
ELISTS. Volume Two.
New York: Doubleday & McClure Company.

Henry James's contribution, "Nathaniel Hawthorne,"
includes pp. 11–32. For original appearance, *see under*
Library of the World's Best Literature, Vol. XII.

Westminster Edition [in red] / [line] / THE /
UNIVERSAL ANTHOLOGY / A Collec-
tion of the Best Literature, Ancient, Mediaeval
and Modern [in red] / With Biographical and
Explanatory Notes [in red] / Edited by / Richard Garnett / Keeper of Printed Books at the
British Museum, London, 1851 to 1899 / Leon
Vallée / Librarian at the Bibliothèque Nationale, Paris, since 1871 / Alois Brandl / Professor
of Literature in the Imperial University of Berlin / [line] / Volume Twenty-Eight [in red] /
Published by / The Clarke Company, Limited,
London / Merrill & Baker, New York Emile
Terquem, Paris / Bibliothek Verlag, Berlin /
[1899]

4to, pp. xxiv. 399, 3 blanks. Plates. Boards, with leather back.

Henry James's contribution, "The Future of the Novel," includes pp. xiii–xxiv.

1901

THE / MAY BOOK / Compiled by Mrs. Aria / In Aid of / Charing Cross Hospital / [quotation, three lines] / London / Macmillan & Co. Limited / 1901.

4to, pp. xii. 164, followed by advertisements, pp. 16. Portraits. Plates. Cloth.

Henry James's contribution, "The Saint's Afternoon," includes pp. 1–10.

An edition de luxe of *The May Book*, limited to one hundred copies, was also issued simultaneously with the regular edition.

See under Italian Hours for a reprinting and extension of this contribution, with the title, "The Saint's Afternoon and Others."

1902

THE LIBRARY OF ORATORY. Chauncey M. Depew. Editor-in-Chief. Nathan Haskell Dole. Caroline Ticknor. Thomas Charles Quinn. Associate Editors. Volume XV.

New York and Chicago: E. R. DuMont.

Henry James's contribution, "James Russell Lowell," includes pp. 368–380. For original appearance, *see under* Library of the World's Best Literature, Vol. XVI.

1904

THE / PROCEEDINGS [in red] / IN COMMEMORATION OF / THE ONE HUNDREDTH ANNIVERSARY / OF THE BIRTH OF / NATHANIEL HAWTHORNE [in red] / Held at / Salem, Massachusetts / June 23, 1904 / [Etched vignette of the Birthplace of Hawthorne] / Salem, Mass. / The Essex Institute [in red] / 1904.

9½ x 6¼ inches, pp. [iv], vi. 116, 2 blanks. Portraits. Boards, with cloth back and paper label.

Henry James's contribution, "Letter" (dated Rye, Sussex, England. June 10, 1904, and addressed to Hon. Robert S. Rantoul), includes pp. 55–62.

The edition of this book was limited to two hundred and fifty numbered copies.

AMERICAN / LITERARY CRITICISM / Selected and Edited, with an / Introductory Essay / By / William Morton Payne, LL.D. / Associate Editor of "The Dial" / Longmans, Green, and Co. / 91 and 93 Fifth Avenue, New York / London and Bombay / 1904.

Crown 8vo, pp. xii. 318, 3 advts., 3 blanks. Cloth. Published in "The Wampum Library of American Literature," Edited by Brander Matthews, Litt.D.

Henry James's contribution, "Sainte-Beuve," pp. 299–318, originally appeared in the *North American Review,*

January, 1880. It was revised by the author for the present publication.

1905

SHORT STORY CLASSICS. (American.) Volume Three. Edited by William Patten.
New York: P. F. Collier & Son.

Henry James's contribution, "The Liar," includes pp. 729–803. For original appearance and first reprinting in a book, *see under* A London Life and Other Tales.

1908

THE WHOLE / FAMILY / A Novel By / Twelve Authors / [ornament in blue] / William Dean Howells / Mary E. Wilkins Freeman / Mary Heaton Vorse / Mary Stuart Cutting / Elizabeth Jordan / John Kendrick Bangs / Henry James / Elizabeth Stuart Phelps / Edith Wyatt / Mary R. Shipman Andrews / Alice Brown Henry Van Dyke / New York and London / Harper & Brothers Publishers / MCMVIII. [The entire title is within a decorative border in blue]

12mo, pp. vi. 315, 1 blank. Illustrations. Cloth.

Henry James's contribution, Chapter VII, "The Married Son," includes pp. 144–184.

1910

IN AFTER DAYS / Thoughts on the Future Life / By / W. D. Howells, Henry James, John / Bigelow, Thomas Wentworth / Higginson,

Henry M. Alden / William Hanna Thomson / Guglielmo Ferrero / Julia Ward Howe / Elizabeth Stuart / Phelps / With Portraits / [publishers' device] / Harper & Brothers Publishers / New York and London / MCMX. [Entire title within a double line border]

12mo, pp. viii. 233, 1 blank. Portraits. Cloth.

Henry James's contribution, "Is There a Life After Death?" includes pp. 199–233.

Originally appeared in *Harper's Bazar*, January–February, 1910.

1911

MODERN MASTERPIECES OF SHORT PROSE FICTION. Edited, with Introduction and Notes by Alice Vinton Waite, Professor of English Language and Composition in Wellesley College, and Edith Mendall Taylor, Instructor in Rhetoric and Composition in Wellesley College.

New York and Chicago: D. Appleton and Company.

Henry James's contribution, "Brooksmith," includes pp. 273–290. For original appearance and first reprinting in a book, *see under* The Lesson of the Master and Other Tales. An Editor's Note states that the text of this contribution is from "the collective and revised edition of Charles Scribner's Sons, by permission of the author."

1914

THE OXFORD BOOK OF AMERICAN ESSAYS Chosen by Brander Matthews Profes-

sor in Columbia University Member of the
American Academy of Arts and Letters.
New York: Oxford University Press, Ameri-
can Branch.

Henry James's contribution, "The Théâtre Français,"
includes pp. 368–393. For original appearance and first
reprinting in a book, *see under* French Poets and Novelists.

1915

THE / BOOK OF FRANCE / In Aid of /
The French Parliamentary Committee's Fund /
For the Relief of the Invaded Departments /
Edited by / Winifred Stephens / Published un-
der the Auspices of an / Honorary Committee
Presided over by / His Excellency Monsieur
Paul Cambon / Macmillan and Co., Limited /
St. Martin's Street, London / Édouard Cham-
pion, Paris / 1915.
4to, pp. xvi. 272. Plates. Cloth.

Henry James's contribution, "France," his remarks at
a meeting of the Committee held on June 9, 1915, includes pp. 1–8. The same book includes "The Saints of
France," a translation by Henry James, pp. 176–182.

1916

THE / BOOK OF THE HOMELESS /
(Le Livre des Sans-Foyer) / Edited by Edith
Wharton / Original Articles in Verse and Prose
/ Illustrations reproduced from Original Paint-

ings & Drawings / [ornament] / The Book is
Sold / For the Benefit of the American Hostels
for Refugees / (With the Foyer Franco-Belge)
/ and of the Children of Flanders Rescue Committee / New York / Charles Scribner's Sons /
MDCCCCXVI.

4to, pp. xxvi. 157, 3 blanks. Decorative title-
pages. Portraits. Plates. Facsimiles. Boards, with
cloth back.

Henry James's contribution, "The Long Wards," includes pp. 115–125.
In addition to the regular edition of this book there are
one hundred and seventy-five copies de luxe. Numbers
1–50 are on French handmade paper. Numbers 51–175
are on Van Gelder paper.

1920

THE GREAT MODERN AMERICAN
STORIES. An Anthology. Compiled and
Edited with an Introduction by William Dean
Howells.

New York: Boni and Liveright.

Henry James's contribution, "A Passionate Pilgrim,"
includes pp. 43–109. For original appearance and first reprinting in a book, see under A Passionate Pilgrim and
Other Tales.

Since 1920 numerous other collections of stories, repre-
senting the work of authors of distinction, have been published, usually for the use of students. In them the following tales of Henry James have been included. A Day
of Days (1866) in *American Short Stories*. Edited by

F. T. Pattee. New York: Duffield & Co. The Visits (1893) in *Short Stories*. Edited by W. T. Hastings, B. C. Clough and K. O. Mason. Boston: Houghton Mifflin Co. The Figure in the Carpet (1896) in *Representative American Short Stories*. Edited by A. Jessup. Boston: Allyn and Bacon. The Friends of the Friends ("The Way It Came," 1896) in *Great Short Stories*. Edited by W. J. and C. W. Dawson. New York: Harper & Brothers; and in *29 Love Stories by Twenty and Nine Authors*. Edited by E. Rhys and C. A. Scott. New York: D. Appleton and Co. The Story in It (1903) in *Great Short Stories of the World*. Edited by B. H. Clark and M. Lieber. New York: Robert M. McBride & Co.

For the original appearance and previous reprintings of each of these tales, *see* the Index.

PART III

Prefaces, Introductions, and a Translation

PREFACES

INTRODUCTIONS AND A

TRANSLATION

1889

THE ODD NUMBER / [line] / Thirteen
Tales / By / Guy de Maupassant [in red] / The
Translation / By Jonathan Sturges / An Introduction / By Henry James / New York / Harper & Brothers, Franklin Square / 1889.

16mo, pp. [ii], xviii. 226, 2 advts., 2 blanks.
Cloth.

Henry James's Introduction, pp. vii–xvii, originally
appeared, under the title "Guy de Maupassant," in *Harper's Weekly*, October 19, 1889.

Plates of this edition were used in printing an English
Edition which has the imprint of James R. Osgood, Mc-
Ilvaine & Co., London, and is in their "Red Letter
Series." The first English Edition is dated 1891.

1891

Alphonse Daudet / [line] / PORT TARAS-
CON [in red] / THE LAST ADVEN-
TURES / OF THE / ILLUSTRIOUS
TARTARIN / Translated / By Henry James
/ Illustrated / by Rossi, Myrbach, Montégut,
Bieler / and Montenard / [publishers' device] /

New York / Harper & Brothers, Franklin Square / 1891. [1890]
8vo, pp. iv. 259, 1 blank, 4 advts. Portrait. Cloth.

Originally appeared in *Harper's Magazine*, June–November, 1890.

In addition to translating this work, Henry James contributed a Translator's Preface, pp. 1–8.

Plates of this edition were used in printing an English Edition, which has the imprint of Sampson Low, Marston & Company, Limited, London. The first English Edition is dated 1892.

SOLDIERS THREE / Setting forth Certain Passages in the Lives / and Adventures of Privates Terence Mulvaney, / Stanley Ortheris, and John Learoyd / With Other Stories / By / Rudyard Kipling / With a Critical Introduction by / Henry James / [quotation, two lines] / Leipzig / Heinemann and Balestier / Limited, London / 1891.

Published in the English Library, Volume LIX. Pp. [vi], xxiv. 273, 1 blank. Wrappers.

Henry James's Critical Introduction includes pp. i–xxi.

The Critical Introduction to *Soldiers Three*, recorded above, was first published in America (1891) as a Critical Introduction to Rudyard Kipling's *Mine Own People*. It was also reprinted, under the title "Mr. Kipling's Early Stories," in *Views and Reviews*.

MINE OWN PEOPLE / By / Rudyard Kipling / Author of / "Plain Tales from the

Hills," "Soldiers Three," "The Phantom /
'Rickshaw," "The Light that Failed," Etc. /
With a Critical Introduction By / Henry James
/ Authorized Edition / New York / United
States Book Company / Successors to / John W.
Lovell Company / 150 Worth St., Cor. Mission
Place / [1891]
 12mo, pp. xxvi. 9–268. Cloth.
 Henry James's Critical Introduction includes pp. vii–
xxvi.
 The stories by Rudyard Kipling in this edition of
Mine Own People are: Bimi, Namgay Doola, The
Recrudescence of Imray, Moti Guj-Mutineer, The Mu-
tiny of the Mavericks, At the End of the Passage, The
Incarnation of Krishna Mulvaney, The Courting of
Dina Shadd, The Man Who Was, A Conference of the
Powers, On Greenhow Hill, Without Benefit of Clergy.
Since the appearance of Henry James's Critical Intro-
duction in this collection of tales, it has been reprinted
frequently in America. In these instances, while "Mine
Own People" may be used for the title of the book, the
group of tales often varies from that in the collection
described above.

1892

THE / AVERAGE / WOMAN / [parallel
with the three lines of the main title of the book
are the five lines of the titles of the three stories]
A Common / Story [ornament] Re / ffey [orna-
ment] Cap / tain My Cap / tain! / By / Wolcott Balestier / With a Biographical / Sketch by
Henry James / London William Heinemann /
MDCCCXCII Bedford Street W.C.

Crown 8vo, pp. xxviii. 188, followed by a tribute to Wolcott Balestier by William Heinemann,
pp. 2, (with verso blank) and publishers' advertisements, pp. 8. Illustrative initials. Cloth.

Henry James's Biographical Sketch, pp. vii–xxviii,
originally appeared in *The Cosmopolitan*, May, 1892.

Mr. Heinemann's tribute to Wolcott Balestier and the
illustrative initials for the three stories are not included
in the American Edition.

THE SAME. *First American Edition.*

THE AVERAGE WOMAN / By / Wolcott
Balestier / with a Preface by Henry James /
New York / United States Book Company / 5
and 7 East Sixteenth Street / [line] / Chicago:
266 & 268 Wabash Ave. / [1892]

12mo, pp. [ii], 260, 2 blanks. Cloth.

Henry James's Preface, pp. 11–34, is the same as his
Biographical Sketch in the English Edition.

1897

LAST STUDIES / By / Hubert Crackanthorpe / Author of / "Sentimental Studies,"
"Wreckage," / "Vignettes," &c. / With a Poem
by Stopford A. Brooke, and / an Appreciation by
Henry James / London / William Heinemann
/ 1897.

Crown 8vo, pp. [ii], xxvi. 224, followed by
publishers' advertisements, pp. 16. Portrait.
Cloth.

Henry James's Appreciation includes pp. xi–xxiii.

1898

IMPRESSIONS / By [ornament] Pierre Loti / With an Introduction by Henry James / Archibald Constable and Co. / Westminster [ornament] MDCCCXCVIII. [The entire title within a decorative design in red]
    Imp. 16mo, pp. iv. 189, 3 blanks. Cloth, with vellum back.

Henry James's Introduction includes pp. 1–21.
Sheets of this edition were used for the American Edition which has the imprint of Brentano, New York. The first American Edition is dated MDCCCC.

1900

The Century Classics / [line] / THE VICAR / OF WAKEFIELD / a Tale / By / Oliver Goldsmith / *Sperate miseri, cavete felices.* / With an Introduction by / Henry James / [publishers' device in black and brown] / New York / The Century Co. / MCM. [The entire title is within a single line border in brown]
    12mo, pp. xxiv. 315, 1 blank. Portrait. Cloth.

Henry James's Introduction includes pp. xi–xx.

1902

[Decorative initial T in green and black, indented and same depth as first five lines of title] THE TWO YOUNG / BRIDES [two ornaments] / Translated from the / French of Honoré / De Balzac [two ornaments] / With a

Critical Introduction by / Henry James [four ornaments] / [ornament] / London: William Heinemann: Mcmii.

Demy 8vo, pp. lii. (with inserted leaf,—Dedication to George Sand,—numbered xlix, verso blank, between pages iv and v) 367, 1 blank. Portrait. Plates. Cloth. Published in "A Century of French Romance," edited by Edmund Gosse.

Henry James's Critical Introduction includes pp. v–xliii.

Reprinted, under the title "Honoré de Balzac, 1902," in *Notes on Novelists With Some Other Notes.*

[Decorative initial M in green and black, indented and same depth as first four lines of title] MADAME BOVARY / [two ornaments] Translated / from the French of / Gustave Flaubert / With a Critical Introduction / by Henry James [three ornaments] / [ornament] / London: William Heinemann: Mcmii.

Demy 8vo, pp. [ii], l. 435, 1 blank. Portrait. Plates. Cloth. Published in "A Century of French Romance," edited by Edmund Gosse.

Henry James's Critical Introduction includes pp. v–xliii.

Reprinted, under the title "Gustave Flaubert," in *Notes on Novelists With Some Other Notes.*

1903

The Novels and Stories of Iván Turgénieff.
MEMOIRS OF A SPORTSMAN. I.

Translated from the Russian by Isabel F. Hapgood. With an Introduction by Henry James.
New York: Charles Scribner's Sons.

Henry James's Introduction includes pp. v–xxxix.
For original appearance and first reprinting in a book,
see under Partial Portraits.
Sheets of this edition were used for the English Edition which has the imprint of J. M. Dent & Co., London. The first English Edition is dated 1905.

1907

THE COMPLETE WORKS / OF / WIL-
LIAM SHAKESPEARE [in red] / with
Annotations and a General / Introduction by
Sidney Lee / Volume XVI / The Tempest [in
red] / With a Special Introduction By / Henry
James / and an Original Frontispiece By / Ger-
trude Demain Hammond / New York / George
D. Sproul [in red] / 1907.

8vo, pp. xxxii. 110, with 2 blank leaves inside
the front cover and 3 blank leaves inside the back
cover. Frontispiece [tissued, with legend etc. in
red]. Boards, with cloth back and paper label.
Published in "The Renaissance Edition of the
Complete Works of Shakespeare."

Henry James's Special Introduction includes pp. ix–
xxxii.
The plates of this edition were also used in printing
Shakespeare's Works for the "University Press Shake-
speare" and "The Harper Edition of Shakespeare's
Works."

1915

PAPERS ON ACTING / II / ART AND
THE ACTOR / By / Constant Coquelin /
Translated by / Abby Langdon Alger / With an
Introduction by / Henry James / [device] /
Printed for the / Dramatic Museum of Colum-
bia University / in the City of New York /
MCMXV.

8vo, pp. vi. 100, 2 blanks. Boards, with paper
label. The second in a series of publications of the
Dramatic Museum of Columbia University.

Henry James's Introduction includes pp. 1–36 and is
dated 1886–1915.

A note on page 91, signed B[rander]. M[atthews].,
states that the Introduction, the substance of which appeared in the *Century Magazine*, January, 1887, was revised by the author especially for this series.

The edition of this book is limited to three hundred
and thirty-three copies.

1916

LETTERS FROM AMERICA / By Rupert
Brooke. / With a Preface by Henry James /
London: Sidgwick & Jackson, Ltd. / 3 Adam
Street, Adelphi. W.C. 1916.

8vo, pp. [iv], xlii. 180, 2 blanks. Portrait.
Cloth, with paper label.

THE SAME. *First American Edition.*

LETTERS FROM AMERICA / By Rupert
Brooke. / With a Preface by Henry James /

New York: Charles Scribner's Sons / 597–599
Fifth Avenue. 1916.

12mo, pp. xlii. 180, 2 blanks. Portrait. Cloth.

Henry James's Preface, said to be "his last piece of
work," includes pp. ix–xlii in both the English and
American editions.

The labels on the back of the first English Edition
were first printed with the date 1915, and later changed
to 1916. On some copies with the 1915 label, the figure 5
was overprinted with a 6.

The American Edition was set up independently from
proofs of the English Edition and shows some variation
from what Rupert Brooke wrote and from what he main-
tained to be correct.

1924

Émile Zola. LA CURÉE. Translated from the
French by Alexander Teixeira De Mattos. With
an Essay by Henry James.

New York: Boni and Liveright.

Henry James's essay, "Émile Zola," includes pp.
v–xli.

For original appearance and first reprinting in a book,
see under Notes on Novelists With Some Other Notes.

The edition of "Six Masterpieces of Émile Zola," of
which this translation comprises one volume, was limited
to 2050 sets.

PART IV

Unpublished Dramatic Works

UNPUBLISHED
DRAMATIC WORKS

1882

DAISY MILLER / A Comedy / By / Henry James Jun. / Not Published / 1882.

7⅛ x 4¾ inches, pp. iv. 139, 1 blank. Wrappers.

This dramatization of *Daisy Miller: A Study* is in three acts and was probably printed for use as a prompt-book. No records of productions have been reported. The author's revision of the stage version, for publication, appeared in the *Atlantic Monthly* and in book form in 1883.

1891

THE AMERICAN / A Comedy in Four Acts / By / Henry James / London / William Heinemann / 1891 / [All rights reserved]

7⅛ x 4¾ inches, pp. iv. 191, 1 blank. Wrappers.

This dramatization of the novel of the same name was produced professionally in London in October, 1891. English critics gave it unusual consideration and in America it was noticed in the *Atlantic Monthly*, December, 1891.

1894

Printed—as Manuscript— / for Private Circulation only. / GUY DOMVILLE / Play in three Acts / by / Henry James. / London: / Printed by J. Miles & Co., 195, Wardour Street, / Oxford Street, W. / 1894.

7¼ x 4⅞ inches, pp. (1–5) 6–79 (printed on one side of page only). Wrappers.

Guy Domville was produced professionally in London in January, 1895. Besides the contemporary opinion in the English press, a criticism in *Harper's Weekly*, March 2, 1895, predicts the failure of the play as a work for the commercial theater.

Some of Henry James's published fiction was first cast in dramatic form. Covering End, which appeared in the *Two Magics* (1898), was originally a one-act play. It was never produced by Miss Ellen Terry, for whom it was written. Long after its appearance in story form the short play was extended and became The High Bid, a three-act comedy, which the Forbes-Robertsons produced in Edinburgh (1908) and in London (1909). Printed copies of the one-act version of Covering End and of The High Bid are unknown.

In 1909 *The Outcry* was written as a comedy in three acts, but its first stage production was not until the year following the author's death. In 1911 Henry James recast the comedy and it was published as a novel. Printed copies of the version for the theater are unknown.

Also, there are records of the dramatizations of the novel, *The Other House*, and of the short story, Owen Wingrave, but no printed copies of them have been reported. *The Other House*, as a tragedy in three acts, was never produced in the theater. Owen Wingrave was converted into a one-act play, The Saloon, and produced by Miss Gertrude Kingston in England in 1910.

PART V

Collective Editions

COLLECTIVE EDITIONS

1883

COLLECTION OF NOVELS AND TALES BY HENRY JAMES. Fourteen Volumes. London: Macmillan and Co.

18mo. Cloth and wrappers.

The Portrait of a Lady. Three volumes.

Roderick Hudson. Two volumes.

The American. Two volumes.

Washington Square.

The Europeans.

Daisy Miller, A Study: Four Meetings: Longstaff's Marriage: Benvolio.

An International Episode: The Pension Beaurepas: The Point of View.

> This is the first publication of *The Point of View* in England. For its original appearance and first reprinting in a book, *see under* The Siege of London and Other Tales.

The Siege of London: Madame de Mauves.

> This is the first publication of *The Siege of London* in a book in England. For its original appearance and first reprinting in a book, *see under* The Siege of London and Other Tales.

The Madonna of the Future: A Bundle of Letters: The Diary of a Man of Fifty: Eugene Pickering.

Confidence.

1907–1917

THE NOVELS AND TALES OF HENRY JAMES. THE NEW YORK

EDITION. Twenty-six Volumes. New York:
Charles Scribner's Sons.

8vo. Various bindings.

Special Prefaces, prepared by the author for Volumes
I–XXIV, are a feature of the New York Edition of the
Novels and Tales.

I. Roderick Hudson.
The author's Preface includes pp. v–xxiii.

II. The American.
The author's Preface includes pp. v–xx.

III.⎫
IV.⎭ The Portrait of a Lady.
The author's Preface includes pp. v–xxi of Volume III.

V.⎫
VI.⎭ The Princess Casamassima.
The author's Preface includes pp. v–xxiii of Volume V.

VII.⎫
VIII.⎭ The Tragic Muse.
The author's Preface includes pp. v–xxii of Volume VII.

IX. The Awkward Age.
The author's Preface includes pp. v–xxiv.

X. The Spoils of Poynton. A London Life. The Chaperon.
The author's Preface includes pp. v–xxiv.

XI. What Maisie Knew. In the Cage. The Pupil.
The author's Preface includes pp. v–xxii.

XII. The Aspern Papers. The Turn of the Screw. The
Liar. The Two Faces.
The author's Preface includes pp. v–xxiv.

XIII. The Reverberator. Madame de Mauves. A Pas-
sionate Pilgrim. The Madonna of the Future. Louisa
Pallant.
The author's Preface includes pp. v–xxi.

XIV. Lady Barbarina. The Siege of London. An International Episode. The Pension Beaurepas. A Bundle of Letters. The Point of View.
    The author's Preface includes pp. v–xxii.

XV. The Lesson of the Master. The Death of the Lion. The Next Time. The Figure in the Carpet. The Coxon Fund.
    The author's Preface includes pp. v–xviii.

XVI. The Author of Beltraffio. The Middle Years. Greville Fane. Broken Wings. The Tree of Knowledge. The Abasement of the Northmores. The Great Good Place. Four Meetings. Paste. Europe. Miss Gunton of Poughkeepsie. Fordham Castle.
    The author's Preface includes pp. v–xii.
    Fordham Castle is here included for the first time in a book. It originally appeared in *Harper's Magazine*, December, 1904.

XVII. The Altar of the Dead. The Beast in the Jungle. The Birthplace. The Private Life. Owen Wingrave. The Friends of the Friends. Sir Edmund Orme. The Real Right Thing. The Jolly Corner. Julia Bride.
    The author's Preface includes pp. v–xxix.
    The Friends of the Friends previously appeared under the title, "The Way It Came."
    The Jolly Corner is here included for the first time in a book. It originally appeared in *The English Review*, December, 1908. For a later reprinting as a separate book, *see under* Uniform Edition of the Tales of Henry James.

XVIII. Daisy Miller. Pandora. The Patagonia. The Marriages. The Real Thing. Brooksmith. The Beldonald Holbein. The Story in It. Flickerbridge. Mrs. Medwin.
    The author's Preface includes pp. v–xxiv.

XIX.⎫
 XX.⎭ The Wings of the Dove.
    The author's Preface includes pp. v–xxiii of Volume XIX.

XXI.⎱
XXII.⎰ The Ambassadors.

> The author's Preface includes pp. v–xxiii of Volume XXI.

XXIII.⎱
XXIV.⎰ The Golden Bowl.

> The author's Preface includes pp. v–xxv of Volume XXIII.

XXV. The Ivory Tower.

> The plates of the first American Edition were used for printing this supplementary volume to the New York Edition of the *Novels and Tales*. The title-page was reset and a frontispiece was added to produce a uniform appearance with the earlier volumes.

XXVI. The Sense of the Past.

> The plates of the first American Edition were used for printing this supplementary volume to the New York Edition of the *Novels and Tales*. The title-page was reset and a frontispiece was added to produce a uniform appearance with the earlier volumes.

Besides the regular issue of the New York Edition of the *Novels and Tales*, a limited edition, comprising 156 numbered sets, was also published.

Volumes I–XXIV, particularly the earlier novels, received careful and scrupulous revision by the author. Beside the Special Prefaces, the New York Edition has other features, including frontispieces in photogravure, which are the author's selection. The book paper of the first twenty-four volumes has the water-mark "H.J." in monogram.

The British demand for the New York Edition was supplied from sheets purchased and bound by Macmillan and Co., London.

A few copies of *The Letters of Henry James*, in two volumes, selected and edited by Percy Lubbock, were bound by the American publishers to match the New York Edition.

Although it was generally announced that the first twenty-four volumes of the New York Edition would include all of the author's fiction that he wished preserved, one tale, Glasses, which he did not include, was revised by him, shortly before his death, as one of the volumes to appear in the Uniform Edition of his tales.

1915–1919

UNIFORM EDITION OF THE TALES OF HENRY JAMES. Fourteen volumes. London: Martin Secker.
   18mo. Cloth.

The Turn of the Screw.

The Aspern Papers.

Daisy Miller.

The Lesson of the Master.

The Death of the Lion.

The Reverberator.

The Beast in the Jungle.

The Coxon Fund.

Glasses.
   The text of this tale was revised by the author for this edition shortly before his death. Glasses was not included by him in the New York—the "Definitive"—Edition of his *Novels and Tales.*

The Pupil.

The Altar of the Dead.

The Figure in the Carpet.

The Jolly Corner.

In the Cage.

   The first twelve of these tales were published in

groups, four each, during 1915–1916. The Jolly Corner was added in 1918 and In the Cage in 1919.

In 1917 an American Edition of the first twelve of these tales was printed by the London publisher, but the steamship to which they were consigned was torpedoed in the English Channel and the books were a total loss. Eventually another issue for America was available and all of the tales in this Uniform Edition have appeared with the imprint of LeRoy Phillips, Boston.

1921–1923

THE NOVELS AND STORIES OF HENRY JAMES. NEW AND COMPLETE EDITION. Thirty-five Volumes. London: Macmillan and Co., Ltd.

Crown 8vo. Pocket Edition, foolscap. 8vo. Cloth.

I. Roderick Hudson.

II. The American.

III. The Europeans.

IV. Confidence.

V. Washington Square.

VI. The Portrait of a Lady. Vol. I.

VII. The Portrait of a Lady. Vol. II.

VIII. The Bostonians. Vol. I.

IX. The Bostonians. Vol. II.

X. The Princess Casamassima. Vol. I.

XI. The Princess Casamassima. Vol. II.

XII. The Tragic Muse. Vol. I.

XIII. The Tragic Muse. Vol. II.

XIV. The Awkward Age.

XV. The Spoils of Poynton. A London Life. The Chaperon.

XVI. What Maisie Knew. In the Cage. The Pupil.

XVII. The Aspern Papers. The Turn of the Screw. The Liar. The Two Faces.

XVIII. The Reverberator. Madame de Mauves. A Passionate Pilgrim. The Madonna of the Future. Louisa Pallant.

XIX. Lady Barbarina. The Siege of London. An International Episode. The Pension Beaurepas. A Bundle of Letters. The Point of View.

XX. The Lesson of the Master. The Death of the Lion. The Next Time. The Figure in the Carpet. The Coxon Fund.

XXI. The Author of Beltraffio. The Middle Years. Greville Fane. Broken Wings. The Tree of Knowledge. The Abasement of the Northmores. The Great Good Place. Four Meetings. Paste. Europe. Miss Gunton of Poughkeepsie. Fordham Castle.

XXII. The Altar of the Dead. The Beast in the Jungle. The Birthplace. The Private Life. Owen Wingrave. The Friends of the Friends. Sir Edmund Orme. The Real Right Thing. The Jolly Corner. Julia Bride.

XXIII. Daisy Miller. Pandora. The Patagonia. The Marriages. The Real Thing. Brooksmith. The Beldonald Holbein. The Story in It. Flickerbridge. Mrs. Medwin.

XXIV. Watch and Ward. Longstaff's Marriage. Eugene Pickering. Benvolio. The Impressions of a Cousin.

XXV. Diary of a Man of Fifty. A New England Winter. The Path of Duty. A Day of Days. A Light Man. Georgina's Reasons. A Landscape Painter. Rose-Agathe. Poor Richard.

XXVI. The Last of the Valerii. Master Eustace. The Romance of Certain Old Clothes. A Most Extraordinary Case. The Modern Warning. Mrs. Temperley. The Solution. Sir Dominick Ferrand. Nona Vincent.

XXVII. Lord Beaupré. The Visits. The Wheel of Time. Collaboration. Glasses. The Great Condition. The Given Case. John Delavoy. The Third Person. The Tone of Time.

XXVIII. Maud Evelyn. The Special Type. The Papers. The Velvet Glove. Mora Montravers. Crapy Cornelia. A Round of Visits. The Bench of Desolation.

XXIX. The Sacred Fount.

XXX. The Wings of the Dove. Vol. I.

XXXI. The Wings of the Dove. Vol. II.

XXXII. The Ambassadors. Vol. I.

XXXIII. The Ambassadors. Vol. II.

XXXIV. The Golden Bowl. Vol. I.

XXXV. The Golden Bowl. Vol. II.

The text used in this collective edition is that of the New York Edition, as far as it goes, and the Critical Prefaces, written for that series, are retained in the volumes to which they refer.

Many stories were omitted from the New York Edition, either because they did not satisfy their author's later taste, or because he could not find room for them in the limited space at his disposal. This edition contains all of the fiction that was published in book form during Henry James's life.

The aspect of a collective edition of much of Henry James's fiction has been contrived by the coöperation of three American publishers:—Houghton Mifflin Co., Harper and Brothers, and Charles Scribner's Sons. They have endeavored to bind the volumes on their lists in a uniform cloth, all 12mo in size. The plates of the New York Edition have been used frequently but, in some instances, the author's Prefaces, designed for that edition, have been omitted.

Ten volumes have been issued by Houghton Mifflin Co.:—*A Passionate Pilgrim and Other Tales. Roderick Hudson. The American. The Europeans. The Portrait of a Lady* (2 volumes). *The Siege of London and Other Tales. The Tragic Muse* (2 volumes). *The Spoils of Poynton.*

Four volumes have been issued by Harper and Brothers:—*Daisy Miller* and *An International Episode. Washington Square. The Awkward Age. The Ambassadors.*

Eleven volumes have been issued by Charles Scribner's Sons:—*What Maisie Knew. The Sacred Fount. The Wings of the Dove* (2 volumes). *The Better Sort. The Golden Bowl* (2 volumes). *The Finer Grain. The Outcry. The Ivory Tower. The Sense of the Past.*

PART VI

Contributions to Periodicals

CONTRIBUTIONS TO
PERIODICALS

1864

NASSAU W. SENIOR'S "Essays on Fiction." (Unsigned review.)

The *North American Review*, October.
Reprinted, under the title "Fiction and Sir Walter Scott," in *Notes and Reviews*, 1921.

1865

HARRIET ELIZABETH PRESCOTT'S "Azarian: An Episode." (Unsigned review.)

The *North American Review*, January.
Reprinted, under the title "Miss Prescott's 'Azarian,'" in *Notes and Reviews*, 1921.

T. ADOLPHUS TROLLOPE'S "Lindisfarn Chase: A Novel." (Unsigned review.)

The *North American Review*, January.
Reprinted, under the title "Lindisfarn Chase," in *Notes and Reviews*, 1921.

[MRS. A. M. C. SEEMULLER'S] "Emily Chester: A Novel." (Unsigned review.)

The *North American Review*, January.
Reprinted in *Notes and Reviews*, 1921.

THE STORY OF A YEAR.

The *Atlantic Monthly*, March.

MATTHEW ARNOLD'S "Essays in Criticism." (Unsigned review.)

The *North American Review*, July.
Reprinted, under the title "Matthew Arnold's Essays," in *Views and Reviews*, 1908.

LOUISA M. ALCOTT'S "Moods." (Unsigned review.)

The *North American Review*, July.
Reprinted, under the title "Miss Alcott's 'Moods,' " in *Notes and Reviews*, 1921.

THE NOBLE SCHOOL OF FICTION. (Unsigned critical notes on Henry Kingsley's novels.)

The *Nation*, July 6.
Reprinted in *Notes and Reviews*, 1921.

ANTHONY TROLLOPE'S "Miss Mackenzie." (Unsigned review.)

The *Nation*, July 13.
Reprinted, under the title "Miss MacKenzie," in *Notes and Reviews*, 1921.

"THE SCHÖNBERG-COTTA FAMILY." (Unsigned review.)

The *Nation*, September 14.
Reprinted in *Notes and Reviews*, 1921.

ANTHONY TROLLOPE'S "Can You Forgive Her?" (Unsigned review.)

The *Nation*, September 28.
Reprinted, under the title "Can You Forgive Her?"
in *Notes and Reviews*, 1921.

[MRS. A. D. T. WHITNEY'S] "The Gayworthys: A Story of Threads and Thrums."
(Unsigned review.)

The *North American Review*, October.
Reprinted, under the title "The Gayworthys," in
Notes and Reviews, 1921.

A FRENCH CRITIC. (Unsigned critical
notes on Edmond Schérer's works.)

The *Nation*, October 12.
Reprinted in *Notes and Reviews*, 1921.

MISS BRADDON. (Unsigned critical notes.)

The *Nation*, November 9.
Reprinted in *Notes and Reviews*, 1921.

MR. WALT WHITMAN. (Unsigned critical notes.)

The *Nation*, November 16.
Reprinted in *Views and Reviews*, 1908.

EUGÉNIE DE GUÉRIN'S JOURNAL.
(Unsigned review.)

The *Nation*, December 14.
Reprinted in *Notes and Reviews*, 1921.

CHARLES DICKENS' "Our Mutual Friend." (Unsigned review.)

The *Nation*, December 21.
Reprinted, under the title "The Limitations of Dickens," in *Views and Reviews*, 1908.

1866

ANTHONY TROLLOPE'S "The Belton Estate." (Unsigned review.)

The *Nation*, January 4.
Reprinted, under the title "The Belton Estate," in *Notes and Reviews*, 1921.

ALGERNON CHARLES SWIN-BURNE'S "Chastelard." (Unsigned review.)

The *Nation*, January 18.
Reprinted, under the title "Swinburne's 'Chastelard,'" in *Notes and Reviews*, 1921.

CHARLES KINGSLEY'S "Hereward, the Last of the English." (Unsigned review.)

The *Nation*, January 25.
Reprinted, under the title "Kingsley's 'Hereward,'" in *Notes and Reviews*, 1921.

A LANDSCAPE PAINTER.

The *Atlantic Monthly*, February.
"Henry W. James" is the name of the author as it appears in the table of contents of Vol. XVII of the *Atlantic Monthly*.

Reprinted in *Stories Revived*, Vol. II, 1885. Also in *A Landscape Painter*, 1919; *Novels and Stories of Henry James*, New and Complete Edition, Vol. XXV.

[MRS. E. R. CHARLES'S] "Winifred Bertram." (Unsigned review.)

The *Nation*, February 1.
Reprinted in *Notes and Reviews*, 1921.

MRS. GASKELL'S "Wives and Daughters: A Novel." (Unsigned review.)

The *Nation*, February 22.
Reprinted, under the title "Mrs. Gaskell," in *Notes and Reviews*, 1921.

HENRY D. SEDLEY'S "Marian Rooke." (Unsigned review.)

The *Nation*, February 22.
Reprinted, under the title "Marian Rooke," in *Notes and Reviews*, 1921.

[MRS. D. M. M. CRAIK'S] "A Noble Life." (Unsigned review.)

The *Nation*, March 1.
Reprinted in *Notes and Reviews*, 1921.

THE WORKS OF EPICTETUS. Edited by Thomas Wentworth Higginson. (Unsigned review.)

The *North American Review*, April.
Reprinted, under the title "Epictetus," in *Notes and Reviews*, 1921.

VICTOR HUGO'S LAST NOVEL. (Unsigned review of "Les Travailleurs de la Mer.")

The *Nation*, April 12.
Reprinted in *Notes and Reviews*, 1921.

A DAY OF DAYS.

The *Galaxy*, June 15.
Reprinted in *Stories Revived*, Vol. I, 1885. Also in *A Landscape Painter*, 1919; *Novels and Stories of Henry James*, New and Complete Edition, Vol. XXV; *American Short Stories*, 1925.

GEORGE ELIOT'S "Felix Holt, The Radical." (Unsigned review.)

The *Nation*, August 16.
Reprinted in *Notes and Reviews*, 1921.

EUGÉNIE DE GUÉRIN'S LETTERS. (Unsigned review.)

The *Nation*, September 13.
Reprinted in *Notes and Reviews*, 1921.

THE NOVELS OF GEORGE ELIOT.

The *Atlantic Monthly*, October.
Reprinted in *Views and Reviews*, 1908.

THE LAST FRENCH NOVEL. (Unsigned review of "Affaire Clémenceau: Mémoire de l'Accusé." By Alexandre Dumas, fils.)

The *Nation*, October 11.
Reprinted in *Notes and Reviews*, 1921.

1867

MY FRIEND BINGHAM.
The *Atlantic Monthly*, March.

MAURICE DE GUÉRIN'S JOURNAL.
(Unsigned review of the English translation.)
The *Nation*, March 7.

RECENT VOLUMES OF POEMS. (Unsigned critical notes.)
The *North American Review*, April.

POOR RICHARD.
The *Atlantic Monthly*, June–August.
Reprinted in *Stories Revived*, Vol. III, 1885. Also in *A Landscape Painter*, 1919; *Novels and Stories of Henry James*, New and Complete Edition, Vol. XXV.

FRANCIS PARKMAN'S "The Jesuits in North America." (Unsigned review.)
The *Nation*, June 6.

HISTORICAL NOVELS. (Unsigned critical notes on novels by the author of "Mary Powell.")
The *Nation*, August 15.

WILLIAM MORRIS' "The Life and Death of Jason: A Poem." (Unsigned review.)
The *North American Review*, October.
Reprinted, under the title "The Poetry of William Morris," in *Views and Reviews*, 1908.

JAMES ANTHONY FROUDE'S "Short Studies on Great Subjects." (Unsigned review.)
The *Nation*, October 31.

MRS. R. H. DAVIS' "Waiting for the Verdict." (Unsigned review.)
The *Nation*, November 21.

ANNE MONCURE CRANE'S "Opportunity: A Novel." (Unsigned review.)
The *Nation*, December 5.

WILLIAM ROUNSEVILLE ALGER'S "The Friendships of Women." (Unsigned review.)
The *Nation*, December 26.

1868

THE STORY OF A MASTERPIECE. (With an illustration by Gaston Fay.)
The *Galaxy*, January–February.

WILLIAM DEAN HOWELLS' "Italian Journeys." (Unsigned review.)
The *North American Review*, January.

THE HUGUENOTS IN ENGLAND. (Unsigned critical notes on Samuel Smiles's "The Huguenots: Their Settlements, Churches

and Industries in England and Ireland" and
Sarah Tytler's "The Huguenot Family in the
English Village.")

The *Nation*, January 9.

PÈRE CHOCARNE'S "The Inner Life of
Father Lacordaire." (Unsigned review of the
English translation.)

The *Nation*, January 16.

"THE MANNERS OF THE DAY" in
Paris. (Unsigned review of Ernest Feydeau's
"La Comtesse de Châlis; ou les Mœurs du
Jour.")

The *Nation*, January 23.

THE ROMANCE OF CERTAIN OLD
CLOTHES.

The *Atlantic Monthly*, February.

Reprinted in *A Passionate Pilgrim and Other Tales*,
1875. Also in *Stories Revived*, Vol. III, 1885; *International Library of Famous Literature*, Vol. XVIII, 1898;
Novels and Stories of Henry James, New and Complete
Edition, Vol. XXVI.

THE PROGRESS OF ANTHROPOL-
OGY. (Unsigned review of A. de Quatrefages'
"Rapport sur les Progrès de l'Anthropologie en
France.")

The *Nation*, February 6.

A MOST EXTRAORDINARY CASE.

The *Atlantic Monthly*, April.
Reprinted in *Stories Revived*, Vol. III, 1885. Also in
A Landscape Painter, 1919; *Novels and Stories of
Henry James*, New and Complete Edition, Vol. XXVI.

PHILIP GILBERT HAMERTON'S
"Contemporary French Painters: An Essay."
(Unsigned review.)

The *North American Review*, April.

TAINE'S ITALY. (Unsigned review of H.
Taine's "Italy: Rome and Naples.")

The *Nation*, May 7.

A PROBLEM. (With an illustration by W. J.
Hennessy.)

The *Galaxy*, June.

SAINTE-BEUVE'S PORTRAITS. (Un-
signed review of the English translation of C. A.
Sainte-Beuve's "Portraits of Celebrated
Women.")

The *Nation*, June 4.

"LINDA TRESSEL." By the author of
"Nina Balatka." (Unsigned review.)

The *Nation*, June 18.

DE GREY: A Romance.

The *Atlantic Monthly*, July.
Reprinted in *Travelling Companions*, 1919.

OSBORNE'S REVENGE.

The *Galaxy*, July.

WILLIAM MORRIS' "The Earthly Paradise: A Poem." (Unsigned review.)

The *North American Review*, July.

COUNT DE FALLOUX'S "Life and Letters of Madame Swetchine." (Unsigned review of the English translation.)

The *North American Review*, July.

GEORGE ELIOT'S "The Spanish Gypsy: A Poem." (Unsigned review.)

The *Nation*, July 2.

WILLIAM MORRIS' "The Earthly Paradise: A Poem." (Unsigned review.)

The *Nation*, July 9.
Reprinted, under the title "The Poetry of William Morris," in *Views and Reviews*, 1908.

GEORGE SAND'S "Mademoiselle Merquem." (Unsigned review.)

The *Nation*, July 16.

OCTAVE FEUILLET'S "Camors: or Life Under the New Empire." (Unsigned review of the English translation.)

The *Nation*, July 30.

GEORGE ELIOT'S "The Spanish Gypsy: A Poem." (Unsigned review.)

The *North American Review*, October.
Reprinted, under the title "The Poetry of George Eliot," in *Views and Reviews*, 1908.

MRS. R. H. DAVIS' "Dallas Galbraith." (Unsigned review.)

The *Nation*, October 22.

"MODERN WOMEN." (Unsigned review of a reprint of a series of articles in the *Saturday Review*.)

The *Nation*, October 22.

1869

PYRAMUS AND THISBE. (Farce.)

The *Galaxy*, April.

A LIGHT MAN.

The *Galaxy*, July.
Reprinted in *Stories by American Authors*, Vol. V, 1884. Also in *Stories Revived*, Vol. I, 1885; *Master Eustace*, 1920; *Novels and Stories of Henry James*, New and Complete Edition, Vol. XXV.

GABRIELLE DE BERGERAC.

The *Atlantic Monthly*, July–September.
Reprinted as a separate book, 1918.

1870

BENJAMIN DISRAELI'S "Lothair." (Unsigned review.)

The *Atlantic Monthly*, August.

SARATOGA. (Unsigned.)

The *Nation*, August 11.
Reprinted in *Portraits of Places*, 1883.

LAKE GEORGE. (Unsigned.)

The *Nation*, August 25.

FROM LAKE GEORGE TO BURLINGTON. (Unsigned.)

The *Nation*, September 1.

NEWPORT. (Unsigned.)

The *Nation*, September 15.
Reprinted in *Portraits of Places*, 1883.

TRAVELLING COMPANIONS.

The *Atlantic Monthly*, November–December.
Reprinted in *Travelling Companions*, 1919.

1871

A PASSIONATE PILGRIM.

The *Atlantic Monthly*, March–April.
Reprinted in *A Passionate Pilgrim and Other Tales*, 1875. Also in *Collection of British Authors*, Vol. 2234, 1884; *Stories Revived*, Vol. II, 1885; *Novels and Tales*

of Henry James, New York Edition, Vol. XIII; *Great Modern American Stories*, 1920; *Novels and Stories of Henry James*, New and Complete Edition, Vol. XVIII.

Translated into French, "Cousin et Cousine," in *Revue des Deux Mondes*, October 1, 1876.

STILL WATERS. (Farce.)

The *Balloon Post*, April 12.

Six numbers of the *Balloon Post* were issued in connection with the fair in Boston, after the Franco-Prussian War, in aid of the destitute people of France.

WATCH AND WARD.

The *Atlantic Monthly*, August–December.

Reprinted as a separate book, 1878. Also in *Novels and Stories of Henry James*, New and Complete Edition, Vol. XXIV.

GUSTAVE DORZ'S "Around a Spring." (Unsigned review of the English translation.)

The *Atlantic Monthly*, August.

AT ISELLA.

The *Galaxy*, August.

Reprinted in *Travelling Companions*, 1919.

QUEBEC. I. (Unsigned.)

The *Nation*, September 28.

Reprinted in *Portraits of Places*, 1883.

QUEBEC. II. (Unsigned.)

The *Nation*, October 5.

Reprinted in *Portraits of Places*, 1883.

NIAGARA. I. (Unsigned.)

The *Nation*, October 12.
Reprinted in *Portraits of Places*, 1883.

NIAGARA. II. (Unsigned.)

The *Nation*, October 19.
Reprinted in *Portraits of Places*, 1883.

JOHN TYNDALL'S "Hours of Exercise in the Alps." (Unsigned review.)

The *Atlantic Monthly*, November.

MASTER EUSTACE.

The *Galaxy*, November.
Reprinted in *Stories Revived*, Vol. III, 1885. Also in *Master Eustace*, 1920; *Novels and Stories of Henry James*, New and Complete Edition, Vol. XXVI.

1872

A CHANGE OF HEART. (Farce.)

The *Atlantic Monthly*, January.

EXHIBITION OF FRENCH PICTURES IN BOSTON. (Unsigned critical notes.)

The *Atlantic Monthly*, January.

H. TAINE'S "Notes sur l'Angleterre." (Unsigned review.)

The *Nation*, January 25.

THÉOPHILE GAUTIER'S "Tableaux de Siége." (Unsigned review.)

The *Nation*, January 25.

PICTURES BY HUNT, GÉROME, ZA-MACOIS AND VIBERT. (Unsigned critical notes.)

The *Atlantic Monthly*, February.

PICTURES BY COLE, DAUBIGNY AND J. APPLETON BROWN. (Unsigned critical notes.)

The *Atlantic Monthly*, March.

NATHANIEL HAWTHORNE'S "French and Italian Journals." (Unsigned review.)

The *Nation*, March 14.

[H.] TAINE'S English Literature. (Review of Van Laun's translation.)

The *Atlantic Monthly*, April.

THE DUTCH AND FLEMISH PIC-TURES IN NEW YORK. (Unsigned critical notes.)

The *Atlantic Monthly*, June.

CHESTER. (Unsigned.)

The *Nation*, July 4.
Reprinted in *Transatlantic Sketches*, 1875. Also in *Foreign Parts*, 1883; *English Hours*, 1905.

LICHFIELD AND WARWICK. (Unsigned.)

The *Nation*, July 25.
Reprinted in *Transatlantic Sketches*, 1875. Also in *Foreign Parts*, 1883; *English Hours*, 1905.

NORTH DEVON. (Unsigned.)

The *Nation*, August 8.
Reprinted in *Transatlantic Sketches*, 1875. Also in *Foreign Parts*, 1883; *English Hours*, 1905.

WELLS AND SALISBURY. (Unsigned.)

The *Nation*, August 22.
Reprinted in *Transatlantic Sketches*, 1875. Also in *Foreign Parts*, 1883; *English Hours*, 1905.

SWISS NOTES. (Unsigned.)

The *Nation*, September 19.
Reprinted in *Transatlantic Sketches*, 1875. Also in *Foreign Parts*, 1883.

FROM CHAMBÉRY TO MILAN. (Unsigned.)

The *Nation*, November 21.
Reprinted in *Transatlantic Sketches*, 1875. Also in *Foreign Parts*, 1883; *Italian Hours*, 1909.

GUEST'S CONFESSION.

The *Atlantic Monthly*, October–November.
Reprinted in *Travelling Companions*, 1919.

1873

THE BETHNAL GREEN MUSEUM.

The *Atlantic Monthly*, January.

HENRI REGNAULT. (Unsigned critical notes on "Correspondance de Henri Regnault.")

The *Nation*, January 2.

THE PARISIAN STAGE. (Unsigned.)

The *Nation*, January 9.
Reprinted in *Transatlantic Sketches*, 1875.

AUGUSTE LAUGEL'S "Italie, Sicile, Bohême: Notes de Voyage." (Unsigned review.)

The *Nation*, February 27.

THE MADONNA OF THE FUTURE.

The *Atlantic Monthly*, March.
Reprinted in *A Passionate Pilgrim and Other Tales*, 1875. Also in *The Madonna of the Future and Other Tales*, Vol. I, 1879; *Collection of British Authors*, Vol. 1881, 1880; *Collection of Novels and Tales by Henry James*, 1883; *Library of the World's Best Literature*, Vol. XIV, 1897; *Novels and Tales of Henry James*, New York Edition, Vol. XIII; *Novels and Stories of Henry James*, New and Complete Edition, Vol. XVIII.
Translated into French, "La Madone de l'Avenir," in *Revue des Deux Mondes*, April 1, 1876.

FROM VENICE TO STRASSBURG. (Unsigned.)

The *Nation*, March 6.

Reprinted in *Transatlantic Sketches*, 1875. In this volume the spelling of the then German city is "Strasburg." Also in *Foreign Parts*, 1883; *Italian Hours*, under the title "Venice: An Early Impression," 1909.

THÉÂTRE DE THÉOPHILE GAUTIER: MYSTÈRES, COMÉDIES, ET BALLETS. (Review.)

The *North American Review*, April.
Reprinted, under the title "Théophile Gautier," in *French Poets and Novelists*, 1878.

THE SWEETHEART OF M. BRISEUX.

The *Galaxy*, June.
Reprinted in *Travelling Companions*, 1919.

THE AFTER-SEASON AT ROME. (Unsigned.)

The *Nation*, June 12.
Reprinted in *Transatlantic Sketches*, 1875. Also in *Italian Hours*, 1909.

A ROMAN HOLIDAY.

The *Atlantic Monthly*, July.
Reprinted in *Transatlantic Sketches*, 1875. Also in *Foreign Parts*, 1883; *Italian Hours*, 1909.

ROMAN RIDES.

The *Atlantic Monthly*, August.
Reprinted in *Transatlantic Sketches*, 1875. Also in *Foreign Parts*, 1883; *Italian Hours*, 1909.

HOMBURG REFORMED. (Unsigned.)

The *Nation*, August 28.
Reprinted in *Transatlantic Sketches*, 1875. Also in *Foreign Parts*, 1883.

VICTOR CHERBULIEZ'S "Meta Holdenis." (Unsigned review.)

The *North American Review*, October.

AN EX-GRAND-DUCAL CAPITAL. (Unsigned.)

The *Nation*, October 9.
Reprinted, under the title "Darmstadt," in *Transatlantic Sketches*, 1875. Also in *Foreign Parts*, 1883.

DUMAS AND GOETHE. (Unsigned critical notes.)

The *Nation*, October 30.

FROM A ROMAN NOTE-BOOK.

The *Galaxy*, November.
Reprinted in *Transatlantic Sketches*, 1875. Also in *Foreign Parts*, 1883; *Italian Hours*, 1909.

ROMAN NEIGHBORHOODS.

The *Atlantic Monthly*, December.
Reprinted in *Transatlantic Sketches*, 1875. Also in *Foreign Parts*, 1883; *Italian Hours*, 1909.

1874

THE AUTUMN IN FLORENCE. (Unsigned.)

The *Nation*, January 1.
Reprinted in *Transatlantic Sketches*, 1875. Also in *Italian Hours*, 1909.

THE LAST OF THE VALERII.

The *Atlantic Monthly*, January.
Reprinted in *A Passionate Pilgrim and Other Tales*, 1875. Also in *Stories Revived*, Vol. III, 1885; *Novels and Stories of Henry James*, New and Complete Edition, Vol. XXVI.
Translated into French, "Le Dernier des Valerius," in *Revue des Deux Mondes*, November 15, 1875.

HOWELLS' POEMS.

The *Independent*, January 8.

A CHAIN OF ITALIAN CITIES.

The *Atlantic Monthly*, February.
Reprinted, under the title "A Chain of Cities," in *Transatlantic Sketches*, 1875. Also in *Foreign Parts*, 1883; *Italian Hours*, 1909.

MME. DE MAUVES.

The *Galaxy*, February–March.
Reprinted in *A Passionate Pilgrim and Other Tales*, 1875. Also in *The Madonna of the Future and Other Tales*, Vol. I, 1879; *Collection of British Authors*, Vol. 1881, 1880; *Collection of Novels and Tales by Henry James*, 1883; *Novels and Tales of Henry James*, New York Edition, Vol. XIII; *Novels and Stories of Henry James*, New and Complete Edition, Vol. XVIII.

JULES SANDEAU'S "Jean de Thommeray."
(Unsigned review.)

The *Nation*, February 5.

PROSPER MÉRIMÉE'S "Dernières Nouvelles." (Unsigned review.)

The *Nation*, February 12.

AN AUTUMN JOURNEY.

The *Galaxy*, April.
Reprinted, under the title "The St. Gothard," in
Transatlantic Sketches, 1875. Also in *Foreign Parts*,
1883; under the title, "The Old Saint-Gothard," in
Italian Hours, 1909.

FRÜHLINGSFLUTHEN. EIN KÖNIG
LEAR DES DORFES. ZWEI NOVEL-
LEN. VON IWAN TURGÉNIEW. (Re-
view.)

The *North American Review*, April.
Reprinted, under the title "Ivan Turgénieff," in
French Poets and Novelists, 1878.

THE LETTERS OF PROSPER MÉRI-
MÉE.

The *Independent*, April 9.
Reprinted, under the title "Mérimée's Letters," in
French Poets and Novelists, 1878.

VICTOR HUGO'S "Ninety-Three." (Unsigned review.)

The *Nation*, April 9.

FLORENTINE NOTES.

The *Independent*, April 23.
Reprinted, as Part II of a contribution under the same title, in *Transatlantic Sketches*, 1875.

FLORENTINE NOTES.

The *Independent*, April 30.
Reprinted, as Part I of a contribution under the same title, in *Transatlantic Sketches*, 1875. Also in *Foreign Parts*, 1883; *Italian Hours*, 1909.

J. FOXCROFT COLE. (Unsigned critical notes.)

The *Atlantic Monthly*, May.

ADINA.

Scribner's Monthly, May–June.
Reprinted in *Travelling Companions*, 1919.

A FLORENTINE GARDEN.

The *Independent*, May 14.
Reprinted, as Part VIII of a contribution under the title "Florentine Notes," in *Transatlantic Sketches*, 1875.

FLORENTINE NOTES.

The *Independent*, May 21.
Reprinted, as Part III of a contribution under the same title, in *Transatlantic Sketches*, 1875. Also as Part II of a contribution under the same title in *Foreign Parts*, 1883.

TUSCAN CITIES. (Unsigned.)

The *Nation*, May 21.
Reprinted in *Transatlantic Sketches*, 1875. Also in *Foreign Parts*, 1883; *Italian Hours*, 1909.

SIENA.

The *Atlantic Monthly*, June.
Reprinted in *Transatlantic Sketches*, 1875. Also in *Foreign Parts*, 1883; *Italian Hours*, 1909.

GUSTAVE FLAUBERT'S "Temptation of St. Anthony." (Unsigned review.)

The *Nation*, June 4.

OLD ITALIAN ART.

The *Independent*, June 11.
Reprinted, as Part IV of a contribution under the title "Florentine Notes," in *Transatlantic Sketches*, 1875. Also as Part III of "Florentine Notes" in *Foreign Parts*, 1883.

FLORENTINE ARCHITECTURE.

The *Independent*, June 18.
Reprinted, as Part V of a contribution under the title "Florentine Notes," in *Transatlantic Sketches*, 1875. Also as Part IV of "Florentine Notes" in *Foreign Parts*, 1883.

AN ITALIAN CONVENT.

The *Independent*, July 2.
Reprinted, as Part VI of a contribution under the title "Florentine Notes," in *Transatlantic Sketches*, 1875.

THE CHURCHES OF FLORENCE.

The *Independent*, July 9.
Reprinted, as Part VII of a contribution under the
title "Florentine Notes," in *Transatlantic Sketches*, 1875.

RAVENNA. (Unsigned.)

The *Nation*, July 9.
Reprinted in *Transatlantic Sketches*, 1875. Also in
Foreign Parts, 1883; *Italian Hours*, 1909.

EMILE MONTÉGUT'S "Souvenirs de Bourgogne." (Unsigned review.)

The *Nation*, July 23.

PROFESSOR FARGO.

The *Galaxy*, August.
Reprinted in *Travelling Companions*, 1919.

A NORTHWARD JOURNEY.

The *Independent*, August 20.
Reprinted, as Part I of a contribution under the title
"The Splügen," in *Transatlantic Sketches*, 1875.

A NORTHWARD JOURNEY.

The *Independent*, August 27.
Reprinted, as Part II of a contribution under the title
"The Splügen," in *Transatlantic Sketches*, 1875.

IN HOLLAND. (Unsigned.)

The *Nation*, August 27.
Reprinted in *Transatlantic Sketches*, 1875. Also in
Foreign Parts, 1883.

IN BELGIUM. (Unsigned.)

The *Nation*, September 3.
Reprinted in *Transatlantic Sketches*, 1875. Also in *Foreign Parts*, 1883.

ANDREW ARCHIBALD PATON'S "Henry Beyle (Otherwise De Stendahl). A Critical and Biographical Study." (Unsigned review.)

The *Nation*, September 17.

THÉOPHILE GAUTIER, Souvenirs Intimes. Par Ernest Feydeau. Histoire du Romantisme, Suivie de Notices Romantiques, Etc. Par Théophile Gautier. (Reviews.)

The *North American Review*, October.

GEORGE ELIOT'S "The Legend of Jubal, and Other Poems." (Unsigned review.)

The *North American Review*, October.
Reprinted, under the title "The Poetry of George Eliot," in *Views and Reviews*, 1908.

EUGENE PICKERING.

The *Atlantic Monthly*, October–November.
Reprinted in *A Passionate Pilgrim and Other Tales*, 1875. Also in *The Madonna of the Future and Other Tales*, Vol. II, 1879; *Collection of British Authors*, Vol. 1888, 1880; *Collection of Novels and Tales by Henry James*, 1883; *Novels and Stories of Henry James*, New and Complete Edition, Vol. XXIV.

Translated into French, "Le Premier Amour d'Eugène Pickering," in *Revue des Deux Mondes*, January 1, 1876. Translated into German, "Eugen Pickering," as a separate book, 1878.

FRANCIS PARKMAN'S "The Old Régime in Canada." (Unsigned review.)

The *Nation*, October 15.

THE DUKE OF MONTPENSIER'S PICTURES AT THE [BOSTON] ATHENÆUM. (Unsigned critical notes.)

The *Atlantic Monthly*, November.

THÉOPHILE GAUTIER'S "A Winter in Russia." (Unsigned review.)

The *Nation*, November 12.

THE SCHOOL FOR SCANDAL AT THE BOSTON MUSEUM. (Unsigned critical notes.)

The *Atlantic Monthly*, December.

JULIAN HAWTHORNE'S "Idolatry: A Romance." (Unsigned review.)

The *Atlantic Monthly*, December.

THOMAS HARDY'S "Far from the Madding Crowd." (Unsigned review.)

The *Nation*, December 24.

J. W. DE FOREST'S "Honest John Vane: A
Story." (Unsigned review.)
The *Nation*, December 31.

1875

BAYARD TAYLOR'S "The Prophet: A
Tragedy." (Unsigned review.)
The *North American Review*, January.

WILLIAM DEAN HOWELLS' "A Fore-
gone Conclusion." (Unsigned review.)
The *North American Review*, January.

PICTURES BY WILDE, BOUGHTON,
J. APPLETON BROWN, MRS. STILL-
MAN AND EGUSQUIZA. (Unsigned
notes.)
The *Atlantic Monthly*, January.

RODERICK HUDSON.
The *Atlantic Monthly*, January–December.

For the first, 1876, and subsequent editions of this
novel in separate book form, *see under* Original Works.

WILLIAM DEAN HOWELLS' "A Fore-
gone Conclusion." (Unsigned review.)
The *Nation*, January 7.

CHARLES NORDHOFF'S "Communistic
Societies." (Unsigned review.)
The *Nation*, January 14.

STOPFORD A. BROOKE'S "Theology in the English Poets." (Unsigned review.)

The *Nation*, January 21.

CHARLES KINGSLEY. (Unsigned note.)

The *Nation*, January 28.

CHARLES C. F. GREVILLE'S "Journal of the Reigns of King George IV, and King William IV." (Unsigned review.)

The *Nation*, January 28.

P. V. N. MYERS' "Remains of Lost Empires." (Unsigned review.)

The *Nation*, January 28.

SIR SAMUEL BAKER'S "Ismailia." (Unsigned review.)

The *Nation*, February 4.

PROFESSOR DAVID MASSON'S ESSAYS. (Unsigned review.)

The *Nation*, February 18.

C. A. SAINTE-BEUVE'S "Premiers Lundis." (Unsigned review.)

The *Nation*, February 18.

CORRESPONDENCE OF WILLIAM ELLERY CHANNING, D.D., AND LUCY AIKIN FROM 1826 TO 1842.

Edited by Anna Letitia Le Breton. (Unsigned review.)

The *Atlantic Monthly*, March.

THEODORE MARTIN'S "Life of His Royal Highness the Prince Consort." (Unsigned review.)

The *Nation*, March 4.

DAVID LIVINGSTONE'S Last Journals. (Unsigned review.)

The *Nation*, March 11.

NOTES ON THE THEATRES. (Unsigned.)

The *Nation*, March 11.

MADAME RISTORI. (Unsigned.)

The *Nation*, March 18.

SIR ARTHUR HELPS'S "Social Pressure." (Unsigned review.)

The *Nation*, March 18.

EZRA STILES GANNETT: Memoir by His Son. (Unsigned review.)

The *Nation*, April 1.

C. M. YONGE'S "Life of John Coleridge Patteson." (Unsigned review.)

The *Nation*, April 8.

C. A. SAINTE-BEUVE'S "English Portraits." (Unsigned review.)

The *Nation*, April 15.

J. THOMSON'S "Indo-China and China." (Unsigned review.)

The *Nation*, April 22.

MACREADY'S   REMINISCENCES. (Unsigned review.)

The *Nation*, April 29.

H. TAINE'S "Notes on Paris." (Unsigned review.)

The *Nation*, May 6.

H. WILLIS BAXLEY'S "Spain." (Unsigned review.)

The *Nation*, May 20.

MR. GEORGE RIGNOLD. (Unsigned note.)

The *Nation*, May 27.

VICTOR CHERBULIEZ'S "Miss Rovel." (Unsigned review of the English translation.)

The *Nation*, June 3.

MR. FRANK DUVENECK. (Unsigned note.)

The *Nation*, June 3.

GEORGE H. CALVERT'S "Essays-Æsthetical." (Unsigned review.)

The *Nation*, June 3.

JAMES ALBERT HARRISON'S "A Group of Poets and Their Haunts." (Unsigned review.)

The *Nation*, June 10.

MRS. HENRY M. FIELD'S "Home Sketches in France, and Other Papers." (Unsigned review.)

The *Nation*, June 10.

LADY DUFF GORDON'S Letters. (Unsigned review.)

The *Nation*, June 17.

CAPTAIN J. A. LAWSON. (Unsigned note.)

The *Nation*, June 24.

PERSONAL REMINISCENCES OF CORNELIA KNIGHT AND THOMAS RAIKES. Edited by R. H. Stoddard. (Unsigned review.)

The *Nation*, June 24.

ON SOME PICTURES LATELY EXHIBITED.

The *Galaxy*, July.

OUIDA'S "Signa: A Story." (Unsigned review.)

The *Nation*, July 1.

ANDREW WYNTER'S "Fruit between the Leaves." (Unsigned review.)

The *Nation*, July 1.

GILBERT HAVEN'S "Our Next-Door Neighbor: A Winter in Mexico." (Unsigned review.)

The *Nation*, July 8.

THÉOPHILE GAUTIER'S "Constantinople." (Unsigned review of Robert Howe Gould's translation.)

The *Nation*, July 15.

HARRIET BEECHER STOWE'S "We and Our Neighbors: Records of an Unfashionable Street." (Unsigned review.)

The *Nation*, July 22.

ALGERNON   CHARLES   SWINBURNE'S Essays and Studies. (Unsigned review.)

The *Nation*, July 29.
Reprinted, under the title "Swinburne's Essays," in *Views and Reviews*, 1908.

BENVOLIO.

The *Galaxy*, August.
Reprinted in *The Madonna of the Future and Other Tales*, Vol. II, 1879. Also in *Collection of British Authors*, Vol. 1888, 1880; *Collection of Novels and Tales by Henry James*, 1883; *Master Eustace*, 1920; *Novels and Stories of Henry James*, New and Complete Edition, Vol. XXIV.

ALBERT RHODES'S "The French at Home." (Unsigned review.)

The *Nation*, August 5.

FRANCES ELLIOT'S "The Italians: A Novel." (Unsigned review.)

The *Nation*, August 12.

"A CHRISTIAN PAINTER OF THE NINETEENTH CENTURY: BEING THE LIFE OF HYPPOLITE FLANDRIN." By the author of "A Dominican Artist," Etc. (Unsigned review.)

The *Nation*, August 26.

MR. TENNYSON'S Drama. (Review of "Queen Mary.")

The *Galaxy*, September.
Reprinted as Part I, under the title "Tennyson's Drama," in *Views and Reviews*, 1908.

A PORTRAIT BY COPLEY. (Unsigned note.)

The *Nation*, September 9.

PORTRAITS BY MR. FRANK DUVE-NECK. (Unsigned note.)

The *Nation*, September 9.

NEW NOVELS. (Unsigned notes.)

The *Nation*, September 23.

T. L. KINGTON-OLIPHANT'S "The Duke and the Scholar, and Other Essays." (Unsigned review.)

The *Nation*, September 30.

THE LETTERS OF MADAME DE SA-BRAN.

The *Galaxy*, October.
Reprinted, under the title "Madame de Sabran," in *French Poets and Novelists*, 1878.

E. S. NADAL'S "Impressions of London Social Life." (Unsigned review.)

The *Nation*, October 7.

LOUISA M. ALCOTT'S "Eight Cousins: or the Aunt-Hill." (Unsigned review.)

The *Nation*, October 14.

JOHN LATOUCHE'S "Travels in Portugal." (Unsigned review.)

The *Nation*, October 21.

THE TWO AMPÈRES.

The *Galaxy*, November.
Reprinted in *French Poets and Novelists*, 1878.

ANDREW WILSON'S "The Abode of Snow: Observations on a Tour from Chinese Tibet to the Indian Caucasus," Etc. (Unsigned review.)

The *Nation*, November 11.

LE DERNIER DES VALERIUS. (Translation of "The Last of the Valerii.")

Revue des Deux Mondes, November 15.
For the original appearance of this tale, *see* the *Atlantic Monthly*, January, 1874.

MR. HENRY IRVING'S Macbeth. (Unsigned note.)

The *Nation*, November 25.

W. W. STORY'S "Nero: an Historical Play." (Unsigned review.)

The *Nation*, November 25.

HONORÉ DE BALZAC.

The *Galaxy*, December.
Reprinted in *French Poets and Novelists*, 1878.

ALVAN S. SOUTHWORTH'S "Four Thousand Miles of African Travel." (Unsigned review.)

The *Nation*, December 2.

"THACKERAYANA: Notes and Anecdotes." (Unsigned review.)
The *Nation*, December 9.

PARIS REVISITED.
The *New York Tribune*, December 11.

LONDON SIGHTS. (Unsigned.)
The *Nation*, December 16.

PARIS AS IT IS.
The *New York Tribune*, December 25.

CHARLES DE MAZADE. (Unsigned note.)
The *Nation*, December 30.

ERNEST RENAN. (Unsigned note.)
The *Nation*, December 30.

GEORGE BARNETT SMITH'S "Poets and Novelists." (Unsigned review.)
The *Nation*, December 30.

1876

LE PREMIER AMOUR D'EUGÈNE PICKERING. (Translation of "Eugene Pickering.")
Revue des Deux Mondes, January 1.
For the original appearance of this tale, *see* the *Atlantic Monthly*, October–November, 1874.

ROSAMOND AND FLORENCE HILL'S "What We Saw in Australia." (Unsigned review.)

The *Nation*, January 6.

A. P. RUSSELL'S "Library Notes." (Unsigned note.)

The *Nation*, January 6.

VERSAILLES AS IT IS.

The *New York Tribune*, January 8.

RECENT NOVELS. (Unsigned notes.)

The *Nation*, January 13.

ROBERT BROWNING'S "Inn Album." (Unsigned review.)

The *Nation*, January 20.
Reprinted, under the title "On a Drama of Robert Browning," in *Views and Reviews*, 1908.

PARISIAN SKETCHES.

The *New York Tribune*, January 22.

PROSPER MÉRIMÉE'S "Lettres à une autre Inconnue." (Unsigned review.)

The *Nation*, January 27.

JOHN BURROUGHS' "Winter Sunshine." (Unsigned review.)

The *Nation*, January 27.
Reprinted, under the title "A Note on John Burroughs," in *Views and Reviews*, 1908.

THE PARISIAN STAGE.

The *New York Tribune*, January 29.

THE MINOR FRENCH NOVELISTS.

The *Galaxy*, February.
Reprinted in part, under the title "Charles de Bernard and Gustave Flaubert," in *French Poets and Novelists*, 1878.

PHILIP GILBERT HAMERTON'S "Round My House: Notes of a Rural Life in France in Peace and War." (Unsigned review.)

The *Nation*, February 3.

PARISIAN LIFE.

The *New York Tribune*, February 5.

PARISIAN TOPICS.

The *New York Tribune*, February 19.

GEORGE ELIOT'S "Daniel Deronda." (Unsigned note.)

The *Nation*, February 24.

PARIS IN ELECTION TIME.

The *New York Tribune*, March 4.

JULIUS RODENBERG'S "England Literary and Social, from a German Point of View." (Unsigned review.)

The *Nation*, March 16.

PARISIAN AFFAIRS.

The *New York Tribune*, March 25.

JULIAN HAWTHORNE'S "Saxon Studies." (Unsigned review.)

The *Nation*, March 30.

THE KING OF POLAND AND MME. GEOFFRIN. (Review of their published letters.)

The *Galaxy*, April.

LA MADONE DE L'AVENIR. (Translation of "The Madonna of the Future.")

Revue des Deux Mondes, April 1.

For the original appearance of this tale, *see* the *Atlantic Monthly*, March, 1873.

PARISIAN TOPICS.

The *New York Tribune*, April 1.

EDMOND SCHÉRER'S "Études Critiques de Littérature." (Unsigned review.)

The *Nation*, April 6.

ART AND LETTERS IN PARIS.

The *New York Tribune*, April 22.

CHARTRES PORTRAYED.

The *New York Tribune*, April 29.
Reprinted, under the title "Chartres," in *Portraits of Places*, 1883.

PARISIAN FESTIVITY.

The *New York Tribune*, May 13.

AUGUSTUS J. C. HARE'S "Cities of Northern and Central Italy." (Unsigned review.)

The *Nation*, May 18.

ART IN FRANCE.

The *New York Tribune*, May 27.

THE AMERICAN.

The *Atlantic Monthly*, June–December; January–May, 1877.
For the first, 1877, and subsequent editions of this novel in separate book form, *see under* Original Works.
For a stage-version of this novel, *see under* Unpublished Dramatic Works.

PARISIAN TOPICS.

The *New York Tribune*, June 17.

THE PARIS SALON. (Unsigned note.)

The *Nation*, June 22.

M. VICTOR CHERBULIEZ ON THE PARIS SALON. (Unsigned note.)

The *Nation*, June 29.

PARISIAN TOPICS.

The *New York Tribune*, July 1.

EUGÈNE FROMENTIN'S "Les Maîtres d'Autrefois: Belgique-Holland." (Unsigned review.)

The *Nation*, July 13.

GEORGE SAND.

The *New York Tribune*, July 22.

M. TAINE'S LETTER UPON GEORGE SAND. (Unsigned note.)

The *Nation*, July 27.

CRAWFORD'S CONSISTENCY.

Scribner's Monthly, August.

SUMMER IN FRANCE.

The *New York Tribune*, August 12.
Reprinted, under the title "Rouen," in *Portraits of Places*, 1883.

A FRENCH WATERING PLACE.

The *New York Tribune*, August 26.
Reprinted, under the title "Etretat," in *Portraits of Places*, 1883.

THE GHOSTLY RENTAL.

Scribner's Monthly, September.

COUSIN ET COUSINE. (Translation of "A Passionate Pilgrim.")

Revue des Deux Mondes, October 1.
For the original appearance of this tale, *see* the *Atlantic Monthly*, March–April, 1871.

IVAN TURGENEF. (Unsigned note.)

The *Nation*, October 5.

HENRI REGNAULT. (Unsigned note.)

The *Nation*, October 26.

M. PARODI'S "Rome Vaincue." (Unsigned note.)

The *Nation*, November 16.

DANIEL DERONDA: a Conversation.

The *Atlantic Monthly*, December.
Reprinted in *Partial Portraits*, 1888.

THE COUNT OF GOBINEAU'S "Nouvelles Asiatiques." (Unsigned review.)

The *Nation*, December 7.

AN AMERICAN AND AN ENGLISH NOVEL. (Unsigned reviews of "Mercy Philbrick's Choice" and Rhoda Broughton's "Joan.")

The *Nation*, December 21.

1877

FROM NORMANDY TO THE PYRE-NEES.

The *Galaxy*, January.
Reprinted in *Portraits of Places*, 1883.

MM. ERCKMANN-CHATRIAN'S "Ami Fritz." (Unsigned note.)

The *Nation*, January 4.

SWINBURNE AND CARLYLE. (Un-signed note.)

The *Nation*, January 11.

MR. TENNYSON'S NEW DRAMA. (Un-signed review of "Harold: a Drama.")

The *Nation*, January 18.
Reprinted as Part II, under the title "Tennyson's Drama," in *Views and Reviews*, 1908.

THE NATIONAL GALLERY. (Unsigned note.)

The *Nation*, January 25.

CHARLES KINGSLEY'S LIFE AND LETTERS. (Unsigned review.)

The *Nation*, January 25.

THE LETTERS OF HONORÉ DE BAL-ZAC. (Review.)

The *Galaxy*, February.
Reprinted, under the title "Balzac's Letters," in *French Poets and Novelists*, 1878.

MAYFAIR AND TRUTH. (Unsigned note on two new weekly journals.)

The *Nation*, February 1.

THE OLD MASTERS AT BURLINGTON HOUSE. (Unsigned note.)

The *Nation*, February 1.

"THE BOOK OF THE PLAY." (Unsigned note.)

The *Nation*, February 8.

MRS. BROWNING'S LETTERS. (Unsigned review.)

The *Nation*, February 15.

G. DE MOLINARI'S "Lettres sur les Etats-Unis et le Canada." (Unsigned review.)

The *Nation*, February 22.

BURLINGTON HOUSE. (Unsigned note.)

The *Nation*, March 15.

D. MACKENZIE WALLACE'S "Russia." (Unsigned review.)

The *Nation*, March 15.

THE PORTRAIT: A Weekly Photograph and Memoir. (Unsigned note on a new periodical.)

The *Nation*, March 22.

THE NINETEENTH CENTURY. (Unsigned note on a new periodical.)

The *Nation*, March 22.

MACMILLAN'S MAGAZINE. (Unsigned note.)

The *Nation*, March 29.

FRED. BURNABY'S "A Ride to Khiva: Travels and Adventures in Central Asia." (Unsigned review.)

The *Nation*, March 29.

THE THÉÂTRE FRANÇAIS.

The *Galaxy*, April.
Reprinted in *French Poets and Novelists*, 1878. Also in *The Oxford Book of American Essays*, 1914.

VERNEY LOVETT CAMERON'S "Across Africa." (Unsigned review.)

The *Nation*, April 5.

THE OXFORD-CAMBRIDGE BOAT RACE. (Unsigned note.)

The *Nation*, April 12.

MISS ELIZABETH THOMPSON. (Unsigned note.)

The *Nation*, April 26.

IVAN TURGENEF'S "Terres Vierges." (Unsigned review.)

The *Nation*, April 26.

THE LONDON THEATRES.

The *Galaxy*, May.

THEODORE MARTIN'S "Life of H. R. H. the Prince Consort." (Unsigned review.)

The *Nation*, May 3.

VICTOR HUGO'S "Légende des Siècles." (Unsigned note.)

The *Nation*, May 3.

EDMOND DE GONCOURT'S "La Fille Elisa." (Unsigned note.)

The *Nation*, May 10.

VICTOR TISSOT'S "Voyage aux Pays Annexés." (Unsigned review.)

The *Nation*, May 17.

THE GROSVENOR GALLERY AND THE ROYAL ACADEMY. (Unsigned notes.)

The *Nation*, May 31.

ALFRED DE MUSSET.

The *Galaxy*, June.
Reprinted in *French Poets and Novelists*, 1878.

[J. FLETCHER'S] "Kismet." (Unsigned review.)

The *Nation*, June 7.

JULIAN HAWTHORNE'S "Garth." (Unsigned review.)

The *Nation*, June 21.

GEORGE SAND.

The *Galaxy*, July.
Reprinted in *French Poets and Novelists*, 1878.

AN ENGLISH EASTER.

Lippincott's Magazine, July.
Reprinted in *Portraits of Places*, 1883. Also in *English Hours*, 1905.

THE PICTURE SEASON IN LONDON.

The *Galaxy*, August.

THREE EXCURSIONS.

The *Galaxy*, September.
Reprinted in part, under the title "Two Excursions," in *Portraits of Places*, 1883. Also in *English Hours*, 1905.

ABBEYS AND CASTLES.

Lippincott's Magazine, October.
Reprinted in *Portraits of Places*, 1883. Also in *English Hours*, 1905.

M. THIERS. (Unsigned note.)

The *Nation*, October 18.

AUGUSTE LAUGEL'S "La France Politique et Sociale." (Unsigned review.)

The *Nation*, October 18.

GEORGE SAND'S "Dernières Pages." (Unsigned note.)

The *Nation*, October 25.

LONDON AT MIDSUMMER.

Lippincott's Magazine, November.
Reprinted in *Portraits of Places*, 1883. Also in *English Hours*, 1905.

IN WARWICKSHIRE.

The *Galaxy*, November.
Reprinted in *Portraits of Places*, 1883. Also in *English Hours*, 1905.

FOUR MEETINGS.

Scribner's Monthly, November.
Reprinted in *Daisy Miller and Other Tales*, 1879.
Also in *Collection of British Authors*, Vol. 1819, 1879;
Collection of Novels and Tales by Henry James, 1883;
The Author of Beltraffio and Other Tales, 1885; *Novels*

and Tales of Henry James, New York Edition, Vol. XVI; *Novels and Stories of Henry James*, New and Complete Edition, Vol. XXI.

Translated in French, "Quatre Rencontres," in *Revue des Deux Mondes*, December 15, 1878. Also in the collective volume, "Daisy Miller, suivi de: Un Épisode international; Quatre rencontres: trois nouvelles," 1886.

Translated into Danish in the collective volume, "Daisy Miller: En Studie." ["En International Episode." "Fire Moder."] 1920.

OCTAVE FEUILLET'S "Les Amours de Philippe." (Unsigned review.)

The *Nation*, November 15.

THE SUBURBS OF LONDON.

The *Galaxy*, December.

1878

PARIS REVISITED.

The *Galaxy*, January.
Reprinted, under the title "Occasional Paris," in *Portraits of Places*, 1883.

A LITTLE TOUR IN FRANCE.

The *Atlantic Monthly*, January.
Reprinted, under the title "Rheims and Laon: A Little Tour," in *Portraits of Places*, 1883.

X. DOUDAN'S NEW VOLUMES. (Unsigned reviews.)

The *Nation*, January 24.

THE OLD MASTERS AT BURLING-TON HOUSE. (Unsigned notes.)

The *Nation*, January 31.

GEORGE FLEMING'S "Mirage." (Unsigned review.)

The *Nation*, March 7.

ITALY REVISITED.

The *Atlantic Monthly*, April.
Reprinted in *Portraits of Places*, 1883. Also in *Italian Hours*, 1909.

RUSKIN'S COLLECTION OF DRAW-INGS BY TURNER. (Unsigned note.)

The *Nation*, April 18.

GEORGE ELIOT. (Unsigned note.)

The *Nation*, April 25.

RECENT FLORENCE.

The *Atlantic Monthly*, May.

THÉODOLINDE.

Lippincott's Magazine, May.
Reprinted, under the title "Rose-Agathe," in *Stories Revived*, Vol. II, 1885. Also in *Novels and Stories of Henry James*, New and Complete Edition, Vol. XXV. Also, under the original title, in *Master Eustace*, 1920.

THE LONDON EXHIBITIONS—The Grosvenor Gallery. (Unsigned note.)

The *Nation*, May 23.

"A SERIES OF TALES FROM BLACK-WOOD'S MAGAZINE." (Unsigned note.)

The *Nation*, May 30.

DAISY MILLER: a Study.

The *Cornhill Magazine*, June–July.

For the first, 1879, and subsequent editions of this tale in separate book form, *see under* Original Works.

Reprinted in *Daisy Miller and Other Tales*, 1879; *Collection of British Authors*, Vol. 1819, 1879; *Collection of Novels and Tales by Henry James*, 1883; *Harper's Franklin Square Library*, No. 303, 1883; *Daisy Miller and An International Episode*, 1892; *Novels and Tales of Henry James*, New York Edition, Vol. XVIII; *Modern Library*, No. 63, 1918; *Daisy Miller and Other Tales*, 1918; *Novels and Stories of Henry James*, New and Complete Edition, Vol. XXIII; *Daisy Miller and An International Episode*, Modern Readers' Series, 1920.

Translated into French, "Daisy Miller, suivi de: Un Épisode international; Quatre rencontres: trois nouvelles," 1886.

Translated into Danish, "Daisy Miller: En Studie." ["En International Episode." "Fire Moder."] 1920.

THEODORE MARTIN'S "Life of His Royal Highness the Prince Consort." (Unsigned review.)

The *Nation*, June 6.

THE LONDON EXHIBITIONS—The Royal Academy. (Unsigned note.)

The *Nation*, June 6.

HENRY IRVING. (Unsigned note.)

The *Nation*, June 13.

AUGUSTUS J. C. HARE'S "Walks in London." (Unsigned review.)

The *Nation*, June 20.

PENSÉES OF JOUBERT. (Unsigned note.)

The *Nation*, June 27.

M. EMILE AUGIER. (Unsigned note.)

The *Nation*, June 27.

THE EUROPEANS.

The *Atlantic Monthly*, July–October.
For the first, 1878, and subsequent editions of this novel in separate book form, *see under* Original Works.

THE BRITISH SOLDIER.

Lippincott's Magazine, August.

LONGSTAFF'S MARRIAGE.

Scribner's Monthly, August.
Reprinted in *The Madonna of the Future and Other Tales*, 1879. Also in *Collection of British Authors*, Vol. 1881, 1880; *Collection of Novels and Tales by Henry*

James, 1883; *Master Eustace*, 1920; *Novels and Stories of Henry James*, New and Complete Edition, Vol. XXIV.

LONDON IN THE DEAD SEASON. (Unsigned.)
The *Nation*, September 26.

AMERICANS ABROAD. (Unsigned.)
The *Nation*, October 3.

IN SCOTLAND—I. (Unsigned.)
The *Nation*, October 10.

IN SCOTLAND—II. (Unsigned.)
The *Nation*, October 24.

THE AFGHAN DIFFICULTY. (Unsigned.)
The *Nation*, November 14.

AN INTERNATIONAL EPISODE.
The *Cornhill Magazine*, December; January, 1879.

For the first, 1879, and a subsequent edition of this tale in separate book form, *see under* Original Works.

Reprinted in *Daisy Miller and Other Tales*, 1879; *Collection of British Authors*, Vol. 1819, 1879; *Collection of Novels and Tales by Henry James*, 1883; *Harper's Franklin Square Library*, No. 303, 1883; *Daisy Miller and An International Episode*, 1892; *Novels and Tales of Henry James*, New York Edition, Vol. XIV; *Modern Library*, No. 63, 1918; *Daisy Miller and Other Tales*, 1918; *Novels and Stories of Henry James*, New and Complete Edition, Vol. XIX; *Daisy Miller and An International Episode*, Modern Readers' Series, 1920.

Translated into French, "Daisy Miller, suivi de: Un Épisode international; Quatre rencontres: trois nouvelles," 1886.

Translated into Danish, "Daisy Miller: En Studie" ["En International Episode." "Fire Moder."] 1920.

FRANCES ANNE KEMBLE'S "Record of a Girlhood." (Unsigned review.)

The *Nation*, December 12.

QUATRE RENCONTRES. (Translation of "Four Meetings.")

Revue des Deux Mondes, December 15.

For the original appearance of this tale, *see Scribner's Monthly*, November, 1877.

MORITZ BUSCH. (Unsigned note.)

The *Nation*, December 19.

WILLIAM BLACK'S "Macleod of Dare." (Unsigned note.)

The *Nation*, December 19.

GERALDINE MACPHERSON'S "Memoirs of Anna Jameson." (Unsigned note.)

The *Nation*, December 19.

WHISTLER. (Unsigned note.)

The *Nation*, December 19.

Reprinted, with a later unsigned note, under the title

"Contemporary Notes on Whistler vs. Ruskin," in *Views and Reviews*, 1908.

THE MEETING OF PARLIAMENT. (Unsigned.)

The *Nation*, December 26.

A. HAYWARD'S "Essays." (Unsigned review.)

The *Nation*, December 26.

1879

THE NEW YEAR IN ENGLAND. (Unsigned.)

The *Nation*, January 23.
Reprinted, under the title "An English New Year," in *Portraits of Places*, 1883. Also in *English Hours*, 1905.

WHISTLER. (Unsigned note.)

The *Nation*, February 13.
Reprinted, with a previous unsigned note, under the title "Contemporary Notes on Whistler vs. Ruskin," in *Views and Reviews*, 1908.

THE WINTER EXHIBITIONS IN LONDON. (Unsigned notes.)

The *Nation*, February 13.

THE REASSEMBLING OF PARLIAMENT. (Unsigned.)

The *Nation*, March 20.

ENGLISH VIGNETTES. (Illustrated.)

Lippincott's Magazine, April.
Reprinted in *Portraits of Places*, 1883. Also in *English Hours*, 1905.

A FRIEND OF LORD BYRON. (Review of Memoir of the Rev. Francis Hodgson, B.D.)

The *North American Review*, April.

THE PENSION BEAUREPAS.

The *Atlantic Monthly*, April.
Reprinted in *Washington Square and Other Tales*, Vol. II, 1881. Also in *Collection of British Authors*, Vol. 1978, 1881; *Collection of Novels and Tales by Henry James*, 1883; *The Siege of London and Other Tales*, 1883; *Novels and Tales of Henry James*, New York Edition, Vol. XIV; *Novels and Stories of Henry James*, New and Complete Edition, Vol. XIX.

AN ENGLISH WINTER WATERING-PLACE. (Unsigned.)

The *Nation*, April 3.
Reprinted in *Portraits of Places*, 1883. Also in *English Hours*, 1905.

THE ROYAL ACADEMY AND THE GROSVENOR GALLERY. (Unsigned notes.)

The *Nation*, May 29.

THE LONDON THEATRES. (Unsigned.)

The *Nation*, June 12.

THE DIARY OF A MAN OF FIFTY.

Harper's Magazine and *Macmillan's Magazine,* July.
Reprinted in *The Madonna of the Future and Other Tales,* Vol. II, 1879. Also in *The Diary of a Man of Fifty and A Bundle of Letters,* 1880; *Collection of British Authors,* Vol. 1888, 1880; *Collection of Novels and Tales by Henry James,* 1883; *Harper's Franklin Square Library,* No. 303, 1883; *Novels and Stories of Henry James,* New and Complete Edition, Vol. XXV.

THE COMÉDIE-FRANÇAISE IN LONDON. (Unsigned.)

The *Nation,* July 31.

CONFIDENCE.

Scribner's Monthly, August–December; January, 1880.
For the first, 1880, and subsequent editions of this novel in separate book form, *see under* Original Works.

A BUNDLE OF LETTERS.

The *Parisian,* December 18.
Reprinted in *The Diary of a Man of Fifty and A Bundle of Letters,* 1880. Also, in separate book form [1880]; *Seaside Library,* No. 702, 1880; *Washington Square and Other Tales,* Vol. II, 1881; *Collection of British Authors,* Vol. 1978, 1881; *Collection of Novels and Tales by Henry James,* 1883; *Harper's Franklin Square Library,* No. 303, 1883; *Novels and Tales of Henry James,* New York Edition, Vol. XIV; *Novels and Stories of Henry James,* New and Complete Edition, Vol. XIX.

1880

SAINTE-BEUVE. (Review of "Correspondance de C. A. Sainte-Beuve.")

The *North American Review*, January.
Reprinted, with revisions by the author, in *American Literary Criticism*, 1904.

NANA. (Review of a novel by Émile Zola.)

The *Parisian*, February 26.

THE LETTERS OF EUGÈNE DELACROIX. (Review.)

The *International Review*, April.

WASHINGTON SQUARE.

The *Cornhill Magazine*, June–November (with illustrations [by George du Maurier]); and *Harper's Magazine*, July–December (without illustrations).
For the first [1880] and subsequent editions of this novel in separate book form, *see under* Original Works.
Reprinted in *Washington Square and Other Tales*, 1881; *Collection of British Authors*, Vols. 1977–1978, 1881.

THE PORTRAIT OF A LADY.

Macmillan's Magazine, October–December; January–November, 1881, and the *Atlantic Monthly*, November–December; January–December, 1881.
For the first, 1881, and subsequent editions of this novel in separate book form, *see under* Original Works.
A translation into French of this novel has been announced for publication by Librairie Stock (Delamain et Boutelleau), Paris.

1882

ALPHONSE DAUDET.

The *Atlantic Monthly*, June.

LONDON PICTURES AND LONDON PLAYS. (Unsigned.)

The *Atlantic Monthly*, August.

VENICE. (Illustrated.)

The *Century Magazine*, November.

Reprinted in *Portraits of Places*, 1883. Also in *Italian Hours*, 1909.

THE POINT OF VIEW.

The *Century Magazine*, December.

Reprinted in *The Siege of London and Other Tales*, 1883. Also in *Collection of Novels and Tales by Henry James*, 1883; *Collection of British Authors*, Vol. 2234, 1884; *Novels and Tales of Henry James*, New York Edition, Vol. XIV; *Novels and Stories of Henry James*, New and Complete Edition, Vol. XIX.

1883

THE SIEGE OF LONDON. (Illustrated by W. Small.)

The *Cornhill Magazine*, January–February.

Reprinted in *The Siege of London and Other Tales*, 1883. Also in *Collection of Novels and Tales by Henry James*, 1883; *Collection of British Authors*, Vol. 2234, 1884; *Novels and Tales of Henry James*, New York Edition, Vol. XIV; *Novels and Stories of Henry James*, New and Complete Edition, Vol. XIX.

Translated into French, "La Conquête de Londres," in *Mercure de France*, November 16–December 1, 1912.

TOMMASO SALVINI.

The *Atlantic Monthly*, March.

DAISY MILLER: A COMEDY.

The *Atlantic Monthly*, April–June.

A version of Daisy Miller for the theater was first printed, "Not Published," in 1882; *see under* Unpublished Dramatic Works.

For the first published, 1883, edition of this comedy in separate book form, *see under* Original Works.

DU MAURIER AND LONDON SOCIETY. (With portrait and illustrations.)

The *Century Magazine*, May.

Reprinted, text only, under the title "George du Maurier," in *Partial Portraits*, 1888.

THE CORRESPONDENCE OF CARLYLE AND EMERSON.

The *Century Magazine*, June.

ANTHONY TROLLOPE. (With portrait-sketch by R. Birch.)

The *Century Magazine*, July.

Reprinted, text only, in *Partial Portraits*, 1888.

EN PROVENCE.

The *Atlantic Monthly*, July–November; February, April–May, 1884.

Reprinted in book form, under the title *A Little Tour*

in France, 1884. Also, with illustrations by Joseph Pennell, 1900. *See under* Original Works.

ALPHONSE DAUDET. (With portrait.)

The *Century Magazine*, August.
Reprinted in *Partial Portraits*, 1888.

THE REMINISCENCES OF ERNEST RENAN. (Unsigned review.)

The *Atlantic Monthly*, August.

THE IMPRESSIONS OF A COUSIN.

The *Century Magazine*, November–December.
Reprinted in *Tales of Three Cities*, 1884. Also in *Novels and Stories of Henry James*, New and Complete Edition, Vol. XXIV.

1884

IVAN TURGÉNIEFF.

The *Atlantic Monthly*, January.
Reprinted in *Partial Portraits*, 1888. Also, as an Introduction to a translation of *The Novels and Stories of Ivan Turgénieff, Memoirs of a Sportsman*, 1903.

MATTHEW ARNOLD. (With portrait.)

The *English Illustrated Magazine*, January.

LADY BARBERINA.

The *Century Magazine*, May–July.
Reprinted in *Tales of Three Cities*, 1884. Also in *Novels and Tales of Henry James*, New York Edition, Vol. XIV; *Novels and Stories of Henry James*, New and Complete Edition, Vol. XIX.

THE AUTHOR OF BELTRAFFIO.

The *English Illustrated Magazine*, June–July.
Reprinted in *Stories Revived*, Vol. I, 1885. Also in
The Author of Beltraffio and Other Tales, 1885; *Novels
and Tales of Henry James*, New York Edition, Vol.
XVI; *Novels and Stories of Henry James*, New and
Complete Edition, Vol. XXI.

A NEW ENGLAND WINTER.

The *Century Magazine*, August–September.
Reprinted in *Tales of Three Cities*, 1884. Also in
Novels and Stories of Henry James, New and Complete
Edition, Vol. XXV.

THE ART OF FICTION.

Longman's Magazine, September.
Reprinted in *The Art of Fiction* [1885]. Also in *Partial Portraits*, 1888; *The Writer*, September, 1899.

THE PATH OF DUTY.

The *English Illustrated Magazine*, December.
Reprinted in *Stories Revived*, Vol. I, 1885. Also in
The Author of Beltraffio and Other Tales, 1885; *Novels
and Stories of Henry James*, New and Complete Edition,
Vol. XXV.

1885

THE BOSTONIANS.

The *Century Magazine*, February–December; January–February, 1886.
For the first, 1886, and subsequent editions of this
novel in separate book form, *see under* Original Works.

GEORGE ELIOT'S LIFE.

The *Atlantic Monthly*, May.
Reprinted in *Partial Portraits*, 1888.

THE PRINCESS CASAMASSIMA.

The *Atlantic Monthly*, September–December; January–October, 1886.
For the first, 1886, and subsequent editions of this novel in separate book form, *see under* Original Works.

1886

WILLIAM DEAN HOWELLS. (With portrait.)

Harper's Weekly, June 19.

EDWIN A. ABBEY. (With portrait.)

Harper's Weekly, December 4.
Reprinted in *Picture and Text*, 1893.

1887

COQUELIN. (With portrait.)

The *Century Magazine*, January.
Reprinted, in substance, as An Introduction to "Art and the Actor" by Constant Coquelin, translated by Abby Langdon Alger, 1915.

CONSTANCE FENIMORE WOOLSON. (With portrait.)

Harper's Weekly, February 12.
Reprinted, under the title "Miss Woolson," in *Partial Portraits*, 1888.

COUSIN MARIA. (With illustrations by C. S. Reinhart.)

Harper's Weekly, August 6, 13, 20.

Reprinted, under the title "Mrs. Temperley," in *A London Life and Other Tales*, Vol. II, 1889. Also in *The English Library*, Vol. 30, 1891; *Novels and Stories of Henry James*, New and Complete Edition, Vol. XXVI.

JOHN S. SARGENT. (With portrait and illustrations.)

Harper's Magazine, October.

Reprinted, text only, in *Picture and Text*, 1893.

THE LIFE OF EMERSON.

Macmillan's Magazine, December.

Reprinted, under the title "Emerson," in *Partial Portraits*, 1888.

1888

LOUISA PALLANT. (With illustrations by C. S. Reinhart.)

Harper's Magazine, February.

Reprinted in *The Aspern Papers and Other Tales*, Vol. II, 1888. Also in *Novels and Tales of Henry James*, New York Edition, Vol. XIII; *Novels and Stories of Henry James*, New and Complete Edition, Vol. XVIII.

THE REVERBERATOR.

Macmillan's Magazine, February–July.

For the first, 1888, and subsequent editions of this tale in separate book form, *see under* Original Works.

Reprinted in *Novels and Tales of Henry James*, New

York Edition, Vol. XIII; *Novels and Stories of Henry James*, New and Complete Edition, Vol. XVIII.

GUY DE MAUPASSANT.

The *Fortnightly Review*, March.
Reprinted in *Partial Portraits*, 1888.

THE ASPERN PAPERS.

The *Atlantic Monthly*, March–May.
Reprinted in *The Aspern Papers and Other Tales*, Vol. I, 1888. Also in *Novels and Tales of Henry James*, New York Edition, Vol. XII; *Novels and Stories of Henry James*, New and Complete Edition, Vol. XVII.

Reprinted as a separate book in *Uniform Edition of the Tales of Henry James*. Also in *New Adelphi Library*, 1926.

Translated into French, "Les Papiers de Jeffroy Aspern," in *Débats*, October 7–December 7, 1920. Also in a collective volume, 1929.

ROBERT LOUIS STEVENSON. (With portrait by J. W. Alexander.)

The *Century Magazine*, April.
Reprinted in *Partial Portraits*, 1888.

PIERRE LOTI.

The *Fortnightly Review*, May.
Reprinted in *Essays in London and Elsewhere*, 1893.

THE LIAR.

The *Century Magazine*, May–June.
Reprinted in *A London Life and Other Tales*, Vol. II, 1889. Also in *The English Library*, Vol. 30, 1891; *Short Story Classics*, Vol. III, 1905; *Novels and Tales*

of Henry James, New York Edition, Vol. XII; *Novels and Stories of Henry James*, New and Complete Edition, Vol. XVII.

TWO COUNTRIES. (With illustrations by C. S. Reinhart.)

Harper's Magazine, June.
Reprinted, under the title "The Modern Warning," in *The Aspern Papers and Other Tales*, Vol. II, 1888. Also in *Novels and Stories of Henry James*, New and Complete Edition, Vol. XXVI.

A LONDON LIFE.

Scribner's Magazine, June–September.
Reprinted in *A London Life and Other Tales*, Vol. I, 1889. Also in *The English Library*, Vol. 30, 1891; *Novels and Tales of Henry James*, New York Edition, Vol. X; *Novels and Stories of Henry James*, New and Complete Edition, Vol. XV.

THE LESSON OF THE MASTER.

The *Universal Review*, July 16–August 15.
Reprinted in *The Lesson of the Master and Other Tales*, 1892. Also in *The English Library*, Vol. 135, 1892; *Novels and Tales of Henry James*, New York Edition, Vol. XV; *Novels and Stories of Henry James*, New and Complete Edition, Vol. XX; *Modern Library*, No. 169, 1930.
Reprinted as a separate book in *Uniform Edition of the Tales of Henry James*.

THE PATAGONIA.

The *English Illustrated Magazine*, August–September.
Reprinted in *A London Life and Other Tales*, Vol.

II, 1889. Also in *The English Library*, Vol. 30, 1891; *Novels and Tales of Henry James*, New York Edition, Vol. XVIII; *Novels and Stories of Henry James*, New and Complete Edition, Vol. XXIII.

THE JOURNAL OF THE BROTHERS DE GONCOURT.

The *Fortnightly Review*, October.
Reprinted in *Essays in London and Elsewhere*, 1893.

LONDON. (With illustrations by Joseph Pennell.)

The *Century Magazine*, December.
Reprinted, text only, in *Essays in London and Elsewhere*, 1893. Also, with illustrations, in *English Hours*, 1905.

1889

THE TRAGIC MUSE.

The *Atlantic Monthly*, January–December; January–May, 1890.
For the first, 1890, and subsequent editions of this novel in separate book form, *see under* Original Works.

AN ANIMATED CONVERSATION.

Scribner's Magazine, March.
Reprinted in *Essays in London and Elsewhere*, 1893.

OUR ARTISTS IN EUROPE. (With portraits and illustrations.)

Harper's Magazine, June.
Reprinted, text only, under the title "Black and White," in *Picture and Text*, 1893.

AFTER THE PLAY.

The *New Review*, June.
Reprinted in *Picture and Text*, 1893.

GUY DE MAUPASSANT.

Harper's Weekly, October 19.
Reprinted as an Introduction to "The Odd Number,"
Thirteen Tales by Guy de Maupassant, 1889.

THE SOLUTION.

The *New Review*, December; January–February,
1890.
Reprinted in *The Lesson of the Master and Other
Tales*, 1892. Also in *The English Library*, Vol. 135,
1892; *Novels and Stories of Henry James*, New and
Complete Edition, Vol. XXVI.

1890

DAUMIER, CARICATURIST. (With portrait and illustrations.)

The *Century Magazine*, January.
Reprinted, text only, under the title "Honoré Daumier," in *Picture and Text*, 1893.

CHARLES S. REINHART. (With portrait.)

Harper's Weekly, June 14.
Reprinted in *Picture and Text*, 1893.

PORT TARASCON: THE LAST ADVENTURES OF THE ILLUSTRIOUS TARTARIN. By Alphonse Daudet. (With

portrait and illustrations.) The Translation, with a Translator's Preface, by Henry James.

Harper's Magazine, June–November.
Reprinted in book form, 1891.

1891

THE PUPIL.

Longman's Magazine, March–April.
Reprinted in *The Lesson of the Master and Other Tales*, 1892. Also in *The English Library*, Vol. 135, 1892; *Novels and Tales of Henry James*, New York Edition, Vol. XI; *Novels and Stories of Henry James*, New and Complete Edition, Vol. XVI.
Reprinted as a separate book in *Uniform Edition of the Tales of Henry James*.
Translated into French, "L'Élève," in *Revue de Paris*, June 1–15, 1921. Also as a separate book, 1929.

THE SCIENCE OF CRITICISM.

The *New Review*, May.
Reprinted, under the title "Criticism," in *Essays in London and Elsewhere*, 1893.

BROOKSMITH. (With illustrative title-sketch.)

Harper's Weekly, May 2.
Reprinted in *The Lesson of the Master and Other Tales*, 1892. Also in *The English Library*, Vol. 135, 1892; *Novels and Tales of Henry James*, New York Edition, Vol. XVIII; *Modern Masterpieces of Short Prose Fiction*, 1911; *Novels and Stories of Henry James*, New and Complete Edition, Vol. XXIII.

ON THE OCCASION OF "HEDDA GABLER."

The *New Review*, June.
Reprinted as part of a paper, under the title "Henrik Ibsen," in *Essays in London and Elsewhere*, 1893.

THE MARRIAGES.

The *Atlantic Monthly*, August.
Reprinted in *The Lesson of the Master and Other Tales*, 1892. Also in *The English Library*, Vol. 135, 1892; *Novels and Tales of Henry James*, New York Edition, Vol. XVIII; *Novels and Stories of Henry James*, New and Complete Edition, Vol. XXIII.

THE CHAPERON.

The *Atlantic Monthly*, November–December.
Reprinted in *The Real Thing and Other Tales*, 1893. Also in *Novels and Tales of Henry James*, New York Edition, Vol. X; *Novels and Stories of Henry James*, New and Complete Edition, Vol. XV.

1892

JAMES RUSSELL LOWELL.

The *Atlantic Monthly*, January.
Reprinted in *Essays in London and Elsewhere*, 1893.

MRS. HUMPHRY WARD. (With portrait.)

The *English Illustrated Magazine*, February.
Reprinted in *Essays in London and Elsewhere*, 1893.

NONA VINCENT. (With illustrations by W. J. Hennessy.)

The *English Illustrated Magazine*, February–March.
Reprinted in *The Real Thing and Other Tales*, 1893.
Also in *Novels and Stories of Henry James*, New and
Complete Edition, Vol. XXVI.

THE PRIVATE LIFE.

The *Atlantic Monthly*, April.
Reprinted in *The Private Life and Other Tales* (*see*
both American and English editions), 1893. Also in
Novels and Tales of Henry James, New York Edition,
Vol. XVII; *Novels and Stories of Henry James*, New
and Complete Edition, Vol. XXII.

LORD BEAUPREY.

Macmillan's Magazine, April–June.
Reprinted, as "Lord Beaupré," in *The Private Life
and Other Tales* (*see* both American and English editions), 1893. Also in *Novels and Stories of Henry James*,
New and Complete Edition, Vol. XXVII.

WOLCOTT BALESTIER. (With portrait.)

The *Cosmopolitan*, May.
Reprinted, as a Biographical Sketch, in *The Average
Woman and Other Tales*, by Wolcott Balestier, 1892.

JERSEY VILLAS. (With illustrations by Ir-
ving R. Wiles.)

The *Cosmopolitan*, July–August.
Reprinted, under the title "Sir Dominick Ferrand," in
The Real Thing and Other Tales, 1893. Also in *Novels
and Stories of Henry James*, New and Complete Edition,
Vol. XXVI.

COLLABORATION.

The *English Illustrated Magazine*, September.
Reprinted in *The Wheel of Time and Other Tales*, 1893. Also in *The Private Life and Other Tales* (English Edition), 1893; *Novels and Stories of Henry James*, New and Complete Edition, Vol. XXVII.

THE GRAND CANAL. (With illustrations by Alexander Zezzos.)

Scribner's Magazine, November.
Reprinted in *The Great Streets of the World*, 1892. Also in *Italian Hours*, 1909.

THE WHEEL OF TIME. (With illustrations by A. B. Wenzell and George Wharton Edwards.)

The *Cosmopolitan*, December; January, 1893.
Reprinted in *The Wheel of Time and Other Tales*, 1893. Also in *The Private Life and Other Tales* (English Edition), 1893; *Novels and Stories of Henry James*, New and Complete Edition, Vol. XXVII.

1893

GUSTAVE FLAUBERT.

Macmillan's Magazine, March.
Reprinted in *Essays in London and Elsewhere*, 1893.

FRANCES ANNE KEMBLE.

Temple Bar, April.
Reprinted in *Essays in London and Elsewhere*, 1893.

THE MIDDLE YEARS.

Scribner's Magazine, May.
Reprinted in *Terminations*, 1895. Also in *Novels and Tales of Henry James*, New York Edition, Vol. XVI; *Novels and Stories of Henry James*, New and Complete Edition, Vol. XXI.

1894

THE DEATH OF THE LION.

The *Yellow Book*, April.
Reprinted in *Terminations*, 1895. Also in *Novels and Tales of Henry James*, New York Edition, Vol. XV; *Novels and Stories of Henry James*, New and Complete Edition, Vol. XX.
Reprinted as a separate book in *Uniform Edition of the Tales of Henry James*.

GEORGE DU MAURIER. (With portrait.)

Harper's Weekly, April 14.

THE COXON FUND.

The *Yellow Book*, July.
Reprinted in *Terminations*, 1895. Also in *Novels and Tales of Henry James*, New York Edition, Vol. XV; *Novels and Stories of Henry James*, New and Complete Edition, Vol. XX.
Reprinted as a separate book in *Uniform Edition of the Tales of Henry James*.

1895

THE NEXT TIME.

The *Yellow Book*, July.
Reprinted in *Embarrassments*, 1896. Also in *Novels*

and Tales of Henry James, New York Edition, Vol.
XV; *Novels and Stories of Henry James*, New and Complete Edition, Vol. XX.

1896

THE FIGURE IN THE CARPET.

Cosmopolis, January–February.

Reprinted in *Embarrassments*, 1896. Also in *Novels and Tales of Henry James*, New York Edition, Vol. XV; *Novels and Stories of Henry James*, New and Complete Edition, Vol. XX; *Representative American Short Stories*, 1923.

Reprinted as a separate book in *Uniform Edition of the Tales of Henry James*.

GLASSES.

The *Atlantic Monthly*, February.

Reprinted in *Embarrassments*, 1896. Also in *Novels and Stories of Henry James*, New and Complete Edition, Vol. XXVII.

Reprinted, with special revision by the author, as a separate book, in *Uniform Edition of the Tales of Henry James*.

ON THE DEATH OF DUMAS THE YOUNGER.

The *New Review*, March.

Reprinted, under the title "Dumas the Younger, 1895," in *Notes on Novelists with Some Other Notes*, 1914.

THE OLD THINGS.

The *Atlantic Monthly*, April–October.

For the first, 1897, edition of this novel in separate

book form, under the title *The Spoils of Poynton, see under* Original Works.

Reprinted, as "The Spoils of Poynton," in *Novels and Tales of Henry James*, New York Edition, Vol. X; *Novels and Stories of Henry James*, New and Complete Edition, Vol. XV.

THE WAY IT CAME.

The *Chap Book*, May 1; and *Chapman's Magazine of Fiction*, May.

Reprinted in *Embarrassments*, 1896. Also, under the title "The Friends of the Friends," in *Novels and Tales of Henry James*, New York Edition, Vol. XVII; *Novels and Stories of Henry James*, New and Complete Edition, Vol. XXII; *Great Short Stories*, 1923; *29 Love Stories by Twenty and Nine Authors*, 1925.

MR. HENRY IRVING'S Production of "Cymbeline." (With portraits of Miss Ellen Terry.)

Harper's Weekly, November 21.

1897

SHE AND HE: Recent Documents.

The *Yellow Book*, January.

On the friendship of George Sand and Alfred de Musset.

Reprinted, under the title "George Sand, 1897," in *Notes on Novelists with Some Other Notes*, 1914.

WHAT MAISIE KNEW.

The *Chap Book*, January 15–August 1; and the *New Review*, February–July.

For the first, 1897, and subsequent editions of this novel in separate book form, *see under* Original Works.

Reprinted in *Novels and Tales of Henry James*, New York Edition, Vol. XI; *Novels and Stories of Henry James*, New and Complete Edition, Vol. XVI.

LONDON. (Dated January 1.)

Harper's Weekly, January 23.

LONDON. (Dated January 15.)

Harper's Weekly, February 6.

Reprinted, under the title "London Notes, January 1897," in *Notes on Novelists with Some Other Notes*, 1914.

LONDON. (Dated February 1.)

Harper's Weekly, February 20.

LONDON. (Dated March 3.)

Harper's Weekly, March 27.

LONDON. (Dated April 3.)

Harper's Weekly, April 24.

LONDON. (Dated May 5.)

Harper's Weekly, June 5.

LONDON. (Dated June 1.)

Harper's Weekly, June 26.

Reprinted, under the title "London Notes, June 1897," in *Notes on Novelists with Some Other Notes*, 1914.

LONDON. (Dated July 1.)

Harper's Weekly, July 31.
Reprinted, under the title "London Notes, July 1897," in *Notes on Novelists with Some Other Notes*, 1914.

LONDON. (Dated July 31.)

Harper's Weekly, August 21.
Reprinted, under the title "London Notes, August 1897," in *Notes on Novelists with Some Other Notes*, 1914.

GEORGE DU MAURIER.

Harper's Magazine, September.

OLD SUFFOLK. (Dated Dunwich, August 31.)

Harper's Weekly, September 25.
Reprinted in *English Hours*, 1905.
By a misprint, the year of the composition of this article, as given in *English Hours*, is "1879."

ALPHONSE DAUDET.

Literature, December 25.

1898

JOHN DELAVOY.

Cosmopolis, January–February.
Reprinted in *The Soft Side*, 1900. Also in *Novels and Stories of Henry James*, New and Complete Edition, Vol. XXVII.

THE TURN OF THE SCREW.

Collier's Weekly, February 5–April 16.

Reprinted in *The Two Magics*, 1898. Also in *Novels and Tales of Henry James*, New York Edition, Vol. XII; *Novels and Stories of Henry James*, New and Complete Edition, Vol. XVII; *Modern Library*, No. 169, 1930.

Reprinted as a separate book in *Uniform Edition of the Tales of Henry James*. Also in *New Adelphi Library*, 1926.

Translated into French, "Le Tour d'Écrou," in a collective volume, 1929.

AMERICAN LETTER. The Question of Opportunities.

Literature, March 26.

THE STORY-TELLER AT LARGE: MR. HENRY HARLAND.

The *Fortnightly Review*, April.

THE LATE JAMES PAYN.

The *Illustrated London News*, April 9.

AMERICAN LETTER.

Literature, April 9.

AMERICAN LETTER.

Literature, April 16.

AMERICAN LETTER.

Literature, April 23.

AMERICAN LETTER.
Literature, April 30.

AMERICAN LETTER.
Literature, May 7.

AMERICAN LETTER.
Literature, May 21.

AMERICAN LETTER.
Literature, May 28.

AMERICAN LETTER.
Literature, June 11.

AMERICAN LETTER.
Literature, June 25.

AMERICAN LETTER.
Literature, July 9.

PROSPER MÉRIMÉE.
Literature, July 23.

THE AWKWARD AGE. A Novel.
Harper's Weekly, October 1–December 31; January 7, 1899.

For the first, 1899, and subsequent editions of this novel in separate book form, *see under* Original Works.

1899

THE GREAT CONDITION.

The *Anglo-Saxon Review*, June.
Reprinted in *The Soft Side*, 1900. Also in *Novels and Stories of Henry James*, New and Complete Edition, Vol. XXVII; *Golden Book Magazine*, December, 1929.

"EUROPE."

Scribner's Magazine, June.
Reprinted in *The Soft Side*, 1900. Also in *Novels and Tales of Henry James*, New York Edition, Vol. XVI; *Novels and Stories of Henry James*, New and Complete Edition, Vol. XXI.

THE PRESENT LITERARY SITUA-TION IN FRANCE.

The *North American Review*, October.

1900

THE GREAT GOOD PLACE.

Scribner's Magazine, January.
Reprinted in *The Soft Side*, 1900. Also in *Novels and Tales of Henry James*, New York Edition, Vol. XVI; *Novels and Stories of Henry James*, New and Complete Edition, Vol. XXI.

THE LETTERS OF ROBERT LOUIS STEVENSON.

The *North American Review*, January.
Reprinted in *Notes on Novelists with Some Other Notes*, 1914.

MAUD-EVELYN.

The *Atlantic Monthly*, April.
Reprinted in *The Soft Side*, 1900. Also in *Novels and Stories of Henry James*, New and Complete Edition, Vol. XXVIII.

MISS GUNTON OF POUGHKEEPSIE.

The *Cornhill Magazine*, May.
Reprinted in *The Soft Side*, 1900. Also in *Novels and Tales of Henry James*, New York Edition, Vol. XVI; *Novels and Stories of Henry James*, New and Complete Edition, Vol. XXI; *Golden Book Magazine*, April, 1925.

THE TONE OF TIME.

Scribner's Magazine, November.
Reprinted in *The Better Sort*, 1903. Also in *Novels and Stories of Henry James*, New and Complete Edition, Vol. XXVII.

BROKEN WINGS. (With illustration by Maurice Greiffenhagen.)

The *Century Magazine*, December.
Reprinted in *The Better Sort*, 1903. Also in *Novels and Tales of Henry James*, New York Edition, Vol. XVI; *Novels and Stories of Henry James*, New and Complete Edition, Vol. XXI.

THE FACES. (With illustrations by Albert Herter.)

Harper's Bazar, December 15.
Reprinted, under the title "The Two Faces," in the *Cornhill Magazine*, June, 1901. Also in *The Better Sort*,

1903; *Novels and Tales of Henry James*, New York Edition, Vol. XII; *Novels and Stories of Henry James*, New and Complete Edition, Vol. XVII.

1901

WINCHELSEA, RYE, AND "DENIS DUVAL." (With illustrations by E. C. Peixotto.)

Scribner's Magazine, January.
Reprinted in *English Hours*, 1905.

MATILDE SERAO.

The *North American Review*, March.
Reprinted in *Notes on Novelists with Some Other Notes*, 1914.

MRS. MEDWIN.

Punch, August 28–September 18.
Reprinted in *The Better Sort*, 1903. Also in *Novels and Tales of Henry James*, New York Edition, Vol. XVIII; *Novels and Stories of Henry James*, New and Complete Edition, Vol. XXIII.

THE BELDONALD HOLBEIN. (With illustrations by Lucius Hitchcock.)

Harper's Magazine, October.
Reprinted in *The Better Sort*, 1903. Also in *Novels and Tales of Henry James*, New York Edition, Vol. XVIII; *Novels and Stories of Henry James*, New and Complete Edition, Vol. XXIII.

EDMOND ROSTAND.

The *Cornhill Magazine* and *The Critic*, November.

1902

BROWNING IN VENICE. Being Recollections by the late Katharine de Kay Bronson, with a Prefatory Note by Henry James.

The *Cornhill Magazine* and *The Critic* [under the title "The Late Mrs. Arthur Bronson"], February.

Reprinted, under the title "Castle Alvisi," in *Italian Hours*, 1909.

FLICKERBRIDGE.

Scribner's Magazine, February.

Reprinted in *The Better Sort*, 1903. Also in *Novels and Tales of Henry James*, New York Edition, Vol. XVIII; *Novels and Stories of Henry James*, New and Complete Edition, Vol. XXIII.

GEORGE SAND: The New Life.

The *North American Review*, April.

Reprinted, under the title "George Sand, 1899," in *Notes on Novelists with Some Other Notes*, 1914.

1903

THE AMBASSADORS.

The *North American Review*, January–December.

For the first, 1903, and subsequent editions of this novel in separate book form, *see under* Original Works.

ÉMILE ZOLA.

The *Atlantic Monthly*, August.

Reprinted in *Notes on Novelists with Some Other Notes*, 1914. Also, as an Introductory Essay to a translation of *La Curée*, by Émile Zola, 1924.

1904

GABRIELE D'ANNUNZIO.

The *Quarterly Review*, April.
Reprinted, under the title "Gabriele D'Annunzio, 1902," in *Notes on Novelists with Some Other Notes*, 1914.

FORDHAM CASTLE.

Harper's Magazine, December.
Reprinted in *Novels and Tales of Henry James*, New York Edition, Vol. XVI. Also in *Novels and Stories of Henry James*, New and Complete Edition, Vol. XXI.

1905

NEW ENGLAND: An Autumn Impression.

The *North American Review*, April–June.
Reprinted in *The American Scene*, 1907.

THE QUESTION OF OUR SPEECH.

Appleton's Booklover's Magazine, August.
Reprinted in *The Question of Our Speech. The Lesson of Balzac. Two Lectures*, 1905.

THE LESSON OF BALZAC.

The *Atlantic Monthly*, August.
Reprinted in *The Question of Our Speech. The Lesson of Balzac. Two Lectures*, 1905.

NEW YORK AND THE HUDSON: A Spring Impression.

The *North American Review*, December.
Reprinted in *The American Scene*, 1907.

1906

NEW YORK: Social Notes. I.

The *North American Review*, January; and the *Fortnightly Review*, February.
Reprinted in *The American Scene*, 1907.

NEW YORK: Social Notes. II.

The *North American Review*, February.
Reprinted in *The American Scene*, 1907.

NEW YORK REVISITED.

Harper's Magazine, February–March, and May.
Reprinted in *The American Scene*, 1907.

BOSTON.

The *North American Review* and the *Fortnightly Review*, March.
Reprinted in *The American Scene*, 1907.

PHILADELPHIA.

The *North American Review* and the *Fortnightly Review*, April.
Reprinted in *The American Scene*, 1907.

WASHINGTON. I.

The *North American Review*, May.
Reprinted in *The American Scene*, 1907.

WASHINGTON. II.

The *North American Review*, June.
Reprinted in *The American Scene*, 1907.

THE SENSE OF NEWPORT. (Illustrated.)

Harper's Magazine, August.
Reprinted in *The American Scene*, 1907.

BALTIMORE.

The *North American Review*, August.
Reprinted in *The American Scene*, 1907.

RICHMOND, VIRGINIA.

The *Fortnightly Review*, November.
Reprinted in *The American Scene*, 1907.

SPEECH OF AMERICAN WOMEN.

Harper's Bazar, November–December.

1907

SPEECH OF AMERICAN WOMEN.

Harper's Bazar, January–February.

MANNERS OF AMERICAN WOMEN.

Harper's Bazar, April–July.

1908

PERLE FAUSSE. (Translation of "Paste.")

Revue Bleue, January 18.
For the original appearance of this tale, *see under*
The Soft Side, 1900.

JULIA BRIDE. (With drawings by W. T. Smedley.)

Harper's Magazine, March–April.

For the first, 1909, edition of this story in separate book form, *see under* Original Works.

Reprinted in *Novels and Tales of Henry James*, New York Edition, Vol. XVII; *Novels and Stories of Henry James*, New and Complete Edition, Vol. XXII.

THE JOLLY CORNER.

The *English Review*, December.

Reprinted in *Novels and Tales of Henry James*, New York Edition, Vol. XVII. Also in *Novels and Stories of Henry James*, New and Complete Edition, Vol. XXII.

Reprinted as a separate book in *Uniform Edition of the Tales of Henry James*.

1909

"THE VELVET GLOVE."

The *English Review*, March.

Reprinted in *The Finer Grain*, 1910. Also in *Novels and Stories of Henry James*, New and Complete Edition, Vol. XXVIII.

MORA MONTRAVERS.

The *English Review*, August–September.

Reprinted in *The Finer Grain*, 1910. Also in *Novels and Stories of Henry James*, New and Complete Edition, Vol. XXVIII.

CRAPY CORNELIA.

Harper's Magazine, October.

Reprinted in *The Finer Grain*, 1910. Also in *Novels*

and Stories of Henry James, New and Complete Edition, Vol. XXVIII.

THE BENCH OF DESOLATION.

Putnam's Magazine, October–December; January, 1910.
Reprinted in *The Finer Grain*, 1910. Also in *Novels and Stories of Henry James*, New and Complete Edition, Vol. XXVIII.

1910

IS THERE A LIFE AFTER DEATH?

Harper's Bazar, January–February.
Reprinted in *In After Days*, 1910.

A ROUND OF VISITS.

The *English Review*, April–May.
Reprinted in *The Finer Grain*, 1910. Also in *Novels and Stories of Henry James*, New and Complete Edition, Vol. XXVIII.

1912

A LETTER TO MR. HOWELLS. (On the occasion of a dinner in New York, March 2, 1912, to celebrate the seventy-fifth birthday of William Dean Howells.)

The *North American Review*, April.

THE NOVEL IN "THE RING AND THE BOOK." (Address delivered before the

Academic Committee of the Royal Society of
Literature in Commemoration of the Centenary
of the Birth of Robert Browning, May 7, 1912.)

The *Quarterly Review*, July.
Reprinted, under the title "The Novel in 'The Ring
and the Book,' 1912," in *Notes on Novelists with Some
Other Notes*, 1914.

LA CONQUÊTE DE LONDRES. (Translation of "The Siege of London.")

Mercure de France, November 16–December 1.
For the original appearance of this tale, *see* the *Cornhill Magazine*, January–February, 1883.

1913

BALZAC. (Review of "Balzac. Par Émile Faguet, de l'Académie Française. Les Grands Écrivains Français.")

The *Times Literary Supplement*, June 19.
Reprinted, under the title "Honoré de Balzac, 1913,"
in *Notes on Novelists with Some Other Notes*, 1914.

1914

THE YOUNGER GENERATION.

The *Times Literary Supplement*, March 19–April 2.
Reprinted, under the title "The New Novel," in *Notes
on Novelists with Some Other Notes*, 1914.

GEORGE SAND, sa vie et ses Œuvres, Vol. III (1838–1848). (Review.)

The *Quarterly Review*, April.

Reprinted, under the title "George Sand, 1914," in *Notes on Novelists with Some Other Notes*, 1914.

1915

MR. AND MRS. JAMES T. FIELDS.

The *Atlantic Monthly*, July.

FOUNDING OF THE "NATION." Recollections of the "Fairies" that attended its Birth.

The *Nation*, July 8.

1916

REFUGEES IN CHELSEA.

The *Times Literary Supplement*, March 23.
Reprinted in *Within the Rim*, 1918.
For a privately printed issue of *Refugees in Chelsea*, *see under* Original Works.

1917

WITHIN THE RIM. (With an Introduction by Elizabeth Asquith, dated March, 1916.)

The *Fortnightly Review*, August.
Reprinted in *Harper's Magazine*, December, 1917.
Also in *Within the Rim*, 1918.

THE MIDDLE YEARS.

Scribner's Magazine, October–November.
For the first, 1917, edition of *The Middle Years* in separate book form, *see under* Original Works.

1920

LES PAPIERS DE JEFFROY ASPERN.
(Translation of "The Aspern Papers.")

Débats, October 7–December 7. Also in a collective volume, 1929.

For the original appearance of this tale, *see* the *Atlantic Monthly*, March–May, 1888.

1921

L'ÉLÈVE. (Translation "The Pupil.")

Revue de Paris, June 1–15. Also as a separate book, 1929.

For the original appearance of this tale, *see Longman's Magazine*, March–April, 1891.

1922

THREE UNPUBLISHED LETTERS AND A MONOLOGUE BY HENRY JAMES.

London Mercury, September.

The first two letters are addressed to H. M. Walbrook, the dramatic critic: the third, referring to the Monologue written for her, is addressed to Miss Ruth Draper.

1924

A HENRY JAMES LETTER.

The *Yale Review*, October.

This letter, prefaced by James McLane, is addressed to Mrs. Lila Cabot Perry.

1925

L'AUTEL DES MORTS. (Translation of "The Altar of the Dead.")

Revue de Paris, November 1. Also as a separate book, 1929.

For the original appearance of this tale, *see under* Terminations, 1895.

Index

A LIST OF TITLES

*With References to the Periodicals and Books in
which they are found.*

INDEX

Booktitles of first and other editions specially described in Parts I–V are in ROMAN CAPITALS. Notes and reviews of books recorded only in Part VI are usually listed by authors.

Epictetus, The Works of, Edited by Thomas Wentworth Higginson.
  1866, the *North American Review*, April.
  1921, Notes and Reviews.
Erckmann-Chatrian, M. M., *Ami Fritz*.
  1877, the *Nation*, January 4.
ESSAYS IN LONDON AND ELSEWHERE (1893).
Etretat.
  1883, Portraits of Places.
  See French Watering-Place, A.
EUGEN PICKERING (1878).
Eugene Pickering.
  1874, the *Atlantic Monthly*, October–November.
  1875, A Passionate Pilgrim and Other Tales.
  1879, The Madonna of the Future and Other Tales. 2 volumes.
  1880, Collection of British Authors, Vol. 1888.
  1880, The Madonna of the Future and Other Tales.
  1883, Collection of Novels and Tales.
  1923, Novels and Stories, New and Complete Edition. Vol. XXIV.
      Translated:—into French, Premier Amour d'Eugène Pickering, Le (1876); into German, Eugen Pickering (1878).
"Europe."
  1899, *Scribner's Magazine*, June.
  1900, The Soft Side.
  1909, Novels and Tales, New York Edition, Vol. XVI.
  1922, Novels and Stories, New and Complete Edition, Vol. XXI.
EUROPEANS, THE (1879).
Europeans, The.
  1878, the *Atlantic Monthly*, July–October.
  1878, London: Macmillan and Co. 2 volumes.
  1878, Collection of British Authors, Vol. 1792.
  1879, Boston: Houghton, Osgood and Company.
  1879, London: Macmillan and Co.
  1883, Collection of Novels and Tales.
  1921, Novels and Stories, New and Complete Edition, Vol. III.
Ex-Grand-Ducal Capital, An.
  1873, the *Nation*, October 9.
  See Darmstadt.
Exhibition of French Pictures in Boston.
  1872, the *Atlantic Monthly*, January.

Faces, The.
  1900, *Harper's Bazar*, December 15.
  See Two Faces, The.
Falloux, Count de, *Life and Letters of Madame Swetchine.*
  1868, the *North American Review*, July.
Felix Holt, The Radical.
  1921, Notes and Reviews.
  See Eliot, George, *Felix Holt, The Radical.*
Feuillet, Octave, *Camors: or Life Under the New Empire.*
  1868, the *Nation*, July 30.
Feuillet, Octave, *Les Amours de Philippe.*
  1877, the *Nation*, November 15.
Few Other Roman Neighbourhoods, A.
  1909, Italian Hours.
Fiction and Sir Walter Scott.
  1921, Notes and Reviews.
  See Senior, Nassau W., *Essays on Fiction.*
Field, Mrs. Henry M., *Home Sketches in France, and Other Papers.*
  1875, the *Nation*, June 10.
Fields, Mr. and Mrs. James T.
  1915, the *Atlantic Monthly*, July.
Figure in the Carpet, The.
  1896, *Cosmopolis*, January–February.
  1896, Embarrassments.
  1909, Novels and Tales, New York Edition, Vol. XV.
  1916, Uniform Edition of the Tales.
  1922, Novels and Stories, New and Complete Edition, Vol. XX.
  1923, Representative American Short Stories.
FINER GRAIN, THE (1910).
Flaubert, Gustave.
  1878, French Poets and Novelists.
  See Minor French Novelists, The.
Flaubert, Gustave.
  1893, *Macmillan's Magazine*, March.
  1893, Essays in London and Elsewhere.
Flaubert, Gustave.
  1914, Notes on Novelists.
  See Madame Bovary (Introduction by Henry James).
Flaubert, Gustave, *Temptation of St. Anthony.*
  1874, the *Nation*, June 4.
Fleming, George, *Mirage.*
  1878, the *Nation*, March 7.

Lake George.
1870, the *Nation*, August 25.
LANDSCAPE PAINTER, A (1919).
Landscape Painter, A.
1866, the *Atlantic Monthly*, February.
1885, Stories Revived, Vol. II.
1919, A Landscape Painter and Other Tales.
1923, Novels and Stories, New and Complete Edition, Vol. XXV.
Last French Novel, The ("Affaire Clémenceau: Mémoire de l'Accusé" by Alexandre Dumas, fils).
1866, the *Nation*, October 11.
1921, Notes and Reviews.
Last of the Valerii, The.
1874, the *Atlantic Monthly*, January.
1875, A Passionate Pilgrim and Other Tales.
1885, Stories Revived, Vol. III.
1923, Novels and Stories, New and Complete Edition, Vol. XXVI.
Translated into French, *see* Dernier des Valerius, Le.
LAST STUDIES (Crackanthorpe) (1897). (Appreciation by Henry James.)
Latouche, John, *Travels in Portugal*.
1875, the *Nation*, October 21.
Laugel, Auguste, *La France Politique et Sociale*.
1877, the *Nation*, October 18.
Laugel, Auguste, *Italie, Sicile, Bohême: Notes de Voyage*.
1873, the *Nation*, February 27.
Lawson, Captain J. A.
1875, the *Nation*, June 24.
Lesson of Balzac, The.
1905, the *Atlantic Monthly*, August.
1905, The Question of Our Speech. The Lesson of Balzac. Two Lectures.
LESSON OF THE MASTER, THE, and Other Tales (1892).
Lesson of the Master, The.
1888, the *Universal Review*, July 16–August 15.
1892, The Lesson of the Master and Other Tales.
1892, English Library, Vol. 135.
1909, Novels and Tales, New York Edition, Vol. XV.
1915, Uniform Edition of the Tales.
1922, Novels and Stories, New and Complete Edition, Vol. XX.
1930, Modern Library, No. 169.

Lowell, James Russell.
  1892, the *Atlantic Monthly*, January.
  1893, Essays in London and Elsewhere.
Lowell, James Russell.
  1897, Library of the World's Best Literature, Vol. XVI.
  1902, The Library of Oratory, Vol. XV.

Macmillan's Magazine.
  1877, the *Nation*, March 29.
Macpherson, Geraldine, *Memoirs of Anna Jameson*.
  1878, the *Nation*, December 19.
Macready's Reminiscences.
  1875, the *Nation*, April 29.
MADAME BOVARY (Flaubert) (1902). (Introduction by
  Henry James.) *See* Flaubert, Gustave.
Madame de Mauves.
  1875, The Passionate Pilgrim and Other Tales.
  1879, The Madonna of the Future and Other Tales. 2 vol-
    umes.
  1880, Collection of British Authors, Vol. 1881.
  1880, The Madonna of the Future and Other Tales.
  1883, Collection of Novels and Tales.
  1908, Novels and Tales, New York Edition, Vol. XIII.
  1922, Novels and Stories, New and Complete Edition, Vol.
    XVIII.
  See Mme. de Mauves.
Madone de l'Avenir, La (Translation of The Madonna of the
  Future).
  1876, *Revue des Deux Mondes*, April 1.
MADONNA OF THE FUTURE, THE, and Other Tales
  (1879).
Madonna of the Future, The.
  1873, the *Atlantic Monthly*, March.
  1875, The Passionate Pilgrim and Other Tales.
  1879, The Madonna of the Future and Other Tales. 2 vol-
    umes.
  1880, Collection of British Authors, Vol. 1881.
  1880, The Madonna of the Future and Other Tales.
  1883, Collection of Novels and Tales.
  1897, Library of the World's Best Literature, Vol. XIV.
  1908, Novels and Tales, New York Edition, Vol. XIII.
  1922, Novels and Stories, New and Complete Edition, Vol.
    XVIII.
  Translated into French, *see* Madone de l'Avenir, La.

Manners of American Women.

1907, *Harper's Bazar*, April–July.

"Manners of the Day in Paris, The" (Feydeau).

1868, the *Nation*, January 23.

"Marian Rooke."

1921, Notes and Reviews.

See Sedley, Henry D., *Marian Rooke*.

Marriages, The.

1891, the *Atlantic Monthly*. August.

1892, The Lesson of the Master and Other Tales.

1892, English Library, Vol. 135.

1909, Novels and Tales, New York Edition, Vol. XVIII.

1922, Novels and Stories, New and Complete Edition, Vol. XXIII.

Married Son, The.

1908, The Whole Family, Chapter VII.

Martin, Theodore, *Life of His Royal Highness the Prince Consort*.

1875, the *Nation*, March 4.

Martin, Theodore, *Life of His Royal Highness the Prince Consort*.

1878, the *Nation*, June 6.

Martin, Theodore, *Life of H.R.H. the Prince Consort*.

1877, the *Nation*, May 3.

Masson, Professor David, Essays.

1875, the *Nation*, February 18.

MASTER EUSTACE, and Other Tales (1920).

Master Eustace.

1871, the *Galaxy*, November.

1885, Stories Revived, Vol. III.

1920, Master Eustace and Other Tales.

1923, Novels and Stories, New and Complete Edition, Vol. XXVI.

Maud-Evelyn.

1900, the *Atlantic Monthly*, April.

1900, The Soft Side.

1923, Novels and Stories, New and Complete Edition, Vol. XXVIII.

Maupassant, Guy de.

1888, the *Fortnightly Review*, March.

1888, Partial Portraits.

Maupassant, Guy de.

1889, *Harper's Weekly*, October 19.

See Odd Number, The.

1883, Portraits of Places.
Question of Opportunities, The (American Letter).
1898, *Literature*, March 26.
QUESTION OF OUR SPEECH, THE. THE LESSON OF BALZAC (Two Lectures) (1905).
Question of Our Speech, The.
1905, *Appleton's Booklover's Magazine*, August.
1905, Question of Our Speech, The—The Lesson of Balzac—Two Lectures.
QUESTION OF THE MIND, THE (1915).
"QUEST OF THE HOLY GRAIL, THE" (1895).

Ravenna.
1874, the *Nation*, July 9.
1875, Transatlantic Sketches.
1883, Foreign Parts.
1909, Italian Hours.
Real Right Thing, The.
1900, The Soft Side.
1909, Novels and Tales, New York Edition, Vol. XVII.
1922, Novels and Stories, New and Complete Edition, Vol. XXII.
REAL THING, THE, and Other Tales (1893).
Real Thing, The.
1893, The Real Thing and Other Tales.
1909, Novels and Tales, New York Edition, Vol. XVIII.
1922, Novels and Stories, New and Complete Edition, Vol. XXIII.
Reassembling of Parliament, The.
1879, the *Nation*, March 20.
Recent Florence.
1878, the *Atlantic Monthly*, May.
Recent Novels.
1876, the *Nation*, January 13.
Recent Volumes of Poems.
1867, the *North American Review*, April.
REFUGEES IN CHELSEA (1920).
Refugees in Chelsea.
1916, the *Times Literary Supplement*, March 23.
1918, Within the Rim and Other Essays.
1920, Chelsea: The Ashendene Press.
Regnault, Henri.
1873, the *Nation*, January 2.
Regnault, Henri.

1878, the *Nation*, April 18.
Russell, A. P., *Library Notes*.
1876, the *Nation*. January 6.

Sabran, Madame de.
1878, French Poets and Novelists.
See Letters of Madame de Sabran, The.
SACRED FOUNT, THE (1901).
Sainte-Beuve.
1880, the *North American Review*, January.
1904, American Literary Criticism.
Sainte-Beuve, C. A., *English Portraits*.
1875, the *Nation*, April 15.
Sainte-Beuve's, C. A., *Premiers Lundis*.
1875, the *Nation*, February 18.
Sainte-Beuve's Portraits.
1868, the *Nation*, June 4.
St. Gothard, The.
1875, Transatlantic Sketches.
1883, Foreign Parts.
See Autumn Journey, An; Old Saint-Gothard, The.
Saint's Afternoon, The.
1901, The May Book.
See Saint's Afternoon and Others, The.
Saint's Afternoon and Others, The.
1909, Italian Hours.
See Saint's Afternoon, The.
Saints of France, The (Translation by Henry James).
1915, The Book of France.
Saloon, The (Stage version of Owen Wingrave). *See* Unpublished Dramatic Works.
Salvini, Tommaso.
1883, the *Atlantic Monthly*, March.
Sandeau, Jules, *Jean de Thommeray*.
1874, the *Nation*, February 5.
Sand, George.
1876, the *New York Tribune*, July 22.
Sand, George.
1877, the *Galaxy*, July.
1878, French Poets and Novelists.
Sand, George (1897).
1914, Notes on Novelists.
See She and He: Recent Documents.
Sand, George (1899).

1914, Notes on Novelists.
See Sand, George, The New Life.
Sand, George (1914).
1914, Notes on Novelists.
See Sand, George, sa Vie et ses Œuvres, Vol. III (1838–1848).
Sand, George, *Dernières Pages.*
1877, the *Nation*, October 25.
Sand, George, *Mademoiselle Merquem.*
1868, the *Nation*, July 16.
Sand, George, The New Life.
1902, the *North American Review*, April.
See Sand, George (1899).
Sand, George, sa Vie et ses Œuvres, Vol. III (1838–1848).
1914, the *Quarterly Review*, April.
See Sand, George (1914).
Saratoga.
1870, the *Nation*, August 11.
1883, Portraits of Places.
Sargent, John S.
1887, *Harper's Magazine*, October.
1893, Picture and Text.
Scherer, Edmond, *Études Critiques de Littérature.*
1876, the *Nation*, April 6.
"Schönberg-Cotta Family, The."
1865, the *Nation*, September 14.
1921, Notes and Reviews.
School for Scandal at the Boston Museum, The.
1874, the *Atlantic Monthly*, December.
Science of Criticism, The.
1891, the *New Review*, May.
See Criticism.
Sedley, Henry D., *Marian Rooke.*
1866, the *Nation*, February 22.
See "Marian Rooke."
Seemuller, Mrs. A. M. C., *Emily Chester: A Novel.*
1865, the *North American Review*, January.
See Emily Chester: A Novel.
Senior, Nassau W., *Essays on Fiction.*
1864, the *North American Review*, October.
See Fiction and Sir Walter Scott.
Sense of Newport, The.
1906, *Harper's Magazine*, August.
1907, The American Scene.